THE
WOMAN
BEHIND THE
MIRROR

THE WOMAN BEHIND THE MIRROR

Finding Inward Satisfaction with Your Outward Appearance

JUDITH COUCHMAN

BROADMAN
& HOLMAN
PUBLISHERS

Nashville, Tennessee

© 1997
by Judy C. Couchman
All rights reserved
Printed in the United States of America

4260-77
0-8054-6077-2

Published by Broadman & Holman Publishers, Nashville, Tennessee
Acquisitions and Development Editor: Janis Whipple
Page Design: Anderson Thomas Design
Typography: TF Designs, Mt. Juliet, Tennessee

Published in association with the literary agency of Alive Communications,
Inc., 1465 Kelly Johnson Blvd., Suite 320, Colorado Springs, CO 80920.

Dewey Decimal Classification: 248.843
Subject Heading: WOMEN/CHRISTIAN LIFE
Library of Congress Card Catalog Number: 97-6535

Unless otherwise stated all Scripture citation is from the Holy Bible, New
International Version, copyright © 1973, 1978, 1984 by International
Bible Society.

Library of Congress Cataloging-in-Publication Data
Couchman, Judy C. 1953-
    The woman behind the mirror : finding satisfaction with your
outward appearance / Judy C. Couchman
        p. cm.
    Includes bibliographical references.
    ISBN 0-8054-6077-2
    1.Christian women—Religious life. 2.Self-acceptance—
Religious aspects— Christianity.   3. Beauty, Personal. I. Title
BV4527.C685   1997
241'.674--dc21—dc21
                                                      97-6535
                                                      CIP

2 3 4 5 01 00 99 98 97

For the women in my family
who inherited The Couchman Body.

By Judith Couchman

The Woman Behind the Mirror

Shaping a Woman's Soul

Designing a Woman's Life Bible Study

Designing a Woman's Life

Lord, Please Help Me to Change

Lord, Have You Forgotten Me?

Why Is Her Life Better Than Mine?

If I'm So Good, Why Don't I Act That Way?

Getting a Grip on Guilt

Compilations by Judith Couchman

Growing Deeper with God (Oswald Chambers)

Anywhere He Leads Me (Corrie ten Boom)

Dare to Believe (Smith Wigglesworth)

Loving God with All Your Heart (Andrew Murray)

A Very Present Help (Amy Carmichael)

CONTENTS

ACKNOWLEDGMENTS

As I continue to write books, I'm touched by the number of people who have taken an interest in my creative work and outreach to women.

For several years these faithful, eternal friends have formed a prayer team to intercede for my life and projects: Charette Barta, Win Couchman, Madalene Harris, Karen Hilt, and Nancy Lemons. Others faithful to pray regularly have been my mother Opal Couchman, her friend Mae Lammers and my sister Shirley Honeywell.

However, during the course of writing this book, even more women have prayed with and for me, especially Janet Guy and Anne Scott. Without the help of these caring women, who understand the power of intercession and spiritual warfare, I might never have finished *The Woman Behind the Mirror*. They kept me moving through the unexpected jolts and disappointments that batter us all, but grow especially intense while trying to accomplish tasks of spiritual value. I am deeply grateful for all of their prayers.

I've also been encouraged by a group of women artists who met bi-monthly for a time to discuss spirituality and creative endeavor. They included Joan Badzik, Anne Elhajoui, Mary Johnson, Beth Lueders, Cindy Robbins, Anne Scott, Naomi Trujillo Smith, Wendy Reis, and occasionally the children or dogs who belong to them. Together we wrestled with how to end creative blocks, find time to pursue talents and passions, earn a decent living from our artistic works and fulfill the God-endowed potential within us. These women have influenced this book in ways they'll never know, and I thank them.

A group of researchers also contributed to this book: Deena Davis, Janet Guy, Melissa Honeywell, Shirley Honeywell, and Claudia Stafford. They scrolled and rifled through computerized card catalogs, rolls of microfiche and piles of books, journals, and magazines at the library to find information on women and body image. I thank them for saving me time and energy, and for ensuring that this book is based on the facts and not just my opinions.

In addition to these women, other friends listened to my process and cheered me on. Mary Brosa showed up with dinners and updates from the outside world. Anne Scott hauled my laundry to her home. Temporary roommate Joan Badzik encouraged me and helped around the house. Lois Rabey met me for quick lunches and ramblings about generating work and getting it done. Deena Davis, Madalene Harris, Nancy Lemons, and Beth Lueders kept updated by phone and e-mail to ask, "How's it going?" And probably without knowing it, editors and managers from various publishing houses bolstered my progress by assuring me of their love and support of my work. These people included Carol Bartley, Gwen Ellis, Bert Ghezzi, Liz Heaney, Rebecca Price, and Dan Rich.

My agent Greg Johnson deserves a big thanks for his part in landing this contract, and for introducing me to Janis Whipple, the editor from Broadman & Holman who believed a spiritual book about body image should be written. Despite a recurrence of cancer, a major medical procedure and an extended recovery time, she insisted on editing this book for me. Janis, you've touched me deeply.

I also am indebted to my mother, Opal Couchman, and sisters, Shirley Honeywell and Barbara Mortensen, for unconditionally loving and supporting me, even when I write about issues that affected our family or them personally. Thank you so much.

Most of all, I am grateful to an abundant God, who fashioned me as a writer and keeps providing me with publishing avenues. He is the one, true Creator.

THE UNBEAUTIFUL ME

Beginning the journey toward self-acceptance.

I lie down, watching my mother, Rachel, swimming in the blue water of the pool. Rachel looks as though she were flying, gently and slowly, through the skies. "You are beautiful."

Rachel doesn't believe me. I can see that from the timid way she glances around. Then she laughs softly and lifts her arms up high in a gesture that is sweet and joyous and rather sexy. I can see why my father Michael couldn't believe his luck when she told him they ought to get married, and why he adored her for over thirty years, until he died.

All the same, she has never believed she has beauty. . . .
　　　　　　　　　　　　　　—Vanessa Redgrave, Actress

As far as the world's standards dictate, I am not a beautiful-looking woman.

During times when my weight has fallen into reasonable submission I've passed for pretty, but even that description grows dubious as I step into the age of fortysomething. This is not a self–pitying admission. It's simply the truth about how I view my physical self. Some good aspects about aging are that you become more realistic about life, more honest with yourself, and hopefully more self-accepting and nurturing.

In my case these qualities arrived in the nick of time because as I grow older gravity is reshaping my appearance. One night I couldn't sleep so I pulled out a new photo album and slid in pictures from the past four years. *Is this really what I look like?* I asked while examining photos of me speaking to a women's group. For a moment I thought the camera had caught me at a distorted angle. Then I realized the other women in these photos looked exactly like themselves, so I couldn't be the only one who consistently appeared older and heavier than reality.

Not long before, I'd scrutinized my undressed face after an unsettling remark from a friend. He's not a mean-spirited person and probably just didn't think before he spoke. Looking at an eight-year-old publicity shot of me he said, "It's time for you to retake that photo. Your face looks more mature now." The next morning I stood a few inches from the mirror, pushing up facial cheeks and wondering about plastic surgery.

Ironically, these days I'm not nearly as fault-finding about my appearance as I used to be. Nor do I worry about body image as some friends do, even the ones who still look indisputably gorgeous. (At age thirty a friend of mine consulted a plastic surgeon about a face lift and he turned her down. "You already look young and beautiful," he said.) In fact, I rarely discuss my appearance, though at times feelings of physical inferiority try to badger me.

Looking for Hope

Whether or not we admit it, most women feel at least some pressure to look good, as if a divine judge peers over our shoulders and into the mirror each morning, poised to deliver a verdict on each imperfection. We know it's silly and unrealistic, this suppressed wish to be physically flawless. We also understand that the standard for "beautiful" changes from year to year and for teenagers, sometimes from day to day. We realize nobody's perfect and as spiritually aware women we believe we shouldn't worry about our appearance. Yet we still do, if not continually at least occasionally.

Is there no hope for us?

God says there's hope and restoration for us all, but not the kind that promises bodily perfection; rather, it's the type that woos us toward self-acceptance, even with that extra body fat or a disfigurement. It's the way the Creator loves and accepts us. Because we are His own, and for Him that is enough. So why isn't it enough for us?

The answer runs deeper than "we've caved into society's pressure" or that parents and teachers didn't build our youthful self-esteem, though these and other influences can contribute to the dilemma. As with many of our struggles, the body-image problem and its resolution reside in the soul, a shadowy place that's more difficult to visit than a workout gym. Yet if we won't explore what's inside of us, we can't truly make peace with what's on the outside. I'm convinced that physical self-acceptance depends on a continuous spiritual out-look.

Making the Journey Together

Please understand. I'm not writing this book because I know all of the answers. I'm writing because like many women I know or receive letters from, I've had to embark on this inward journey toward self-acceptance. I've needed to celebrate the God-endowed face and body that is uniquely and utterly mine. And if you desire the same acceptance for yourself, let's travel these pages together.

First, by sharing my personal journey, other women's stories, and the facts and opinions of body-image experts and researchers, we'll explore why most women struggle with accepting their appearance. When I began writing this book I planned on committing one chapter to the influences that affect body image. Instead, I devoted almost three chapters to the question, "Why are so many of us self-critical about our looks?"

The deeper I dug, the more convinced I became that understanding a negative body image isn't a matter of identifying a few people who color(ed) our self-perception. More accurately, this dissatisfaction emerges from a complex web of factors, including peer pressure, media myths, family attitudes, personal beliefs, and cultural expectations. These influences usually neglect our souls and interestingly, chapters one through three became a presentation of the body-image crisis as it exists, without much spiritual commentary on my part.

For me, these pages grew into a metaphor for how our culture, including Christian women, views physical bodies from the world's rather than God's vantage-point. So as we move through the beginning of this book, use it as a source of information and a vehicle for self-assessment, asking, "Who and what has affected my opinion of my appearance?"

Beginning with chapter four, "Reflections of Eve," we'll examine how God's redemptive relationship with us can heal our wounds and reshape our body image. Please note, I'm not saying, "change how we look" or "provide step-by-step instructions" for eradicating this struggle once and for all. Rather, we'll explore the basic personal issues we need to confront and the biblical principles we can apply to stop focusing on what we look like and start concentrating on who God created us to be. We'll discover how He transforms the empty, pagan priorities of body preoccupation into the fulfilling, sacred work of beautifying the soul.

In other words, we'll stop focusing on the woman in front of the mirror, and begin to love and appreciate, in a proverbial sense, the woman standing behind it. Viewing her from God's perspective, we'll delight in how lovely and captivating she can be.

According to ancient wisdom, "Charm is deceptive, and beauty is fleeting; but a woman who fears the Lord is to be praised" (Prov. 31:30). With the truth of God's Word and the willingness to look within, I pray we will embrace this message not only for ourselves, but for our spiritual sisters of this generation.

—*Judith Couchman*

Chapter One

MIRROR IMAGES

Looking and disliking the woman we see.

I felt I was being mistaken for someone else. The person in the mirror was an impostor—why couldn't anyone else see this?

The only solution I could think of was to stop looking. It wasn't easy. I'd never suspected how omnipresent our own images are. I became an expert on the reflected image, its numerous tricks and wiles, how it can spring up at you from a glass tabletop, a well-polished door handle, a darkened window, a pair of sunglasses, a restaurant's otherwise magnificent brass-plated coffee machine sitting innocently by the cash register.

—Lucy Grealy, Face Cancer Patient

Most of my life I've hated mirrors.

Mirrors, and photographs. They reflect my physicality, and much of my life I've been tempted to discredit its value. Most of my distaste centered on an up-and-down struggle with my weight, which at birth captured many people's worried attention.

I entered the world two months before the due date and my family claims that was the only time I arrived early for anything. Also, it was the one time I qualified to be called thin. Actually, I was perilously underweight, a premature baby brushing the scales with three pounds and ten ounces. This earned me a one-month stay in an incubator, apart from my mother and subjected to spontaneous remarks about my appearance.

"Oh, look how wrinkled and skinny she is!"

"I could fit her in the palm of my hand."

"She looks like a little old man with no eyebrows or fingernails."

"I don't think she's going to make it."

Most people don't believe newborns can understand what adults say, but I'm prone to think they can, or at least that infants absorb the atmosphere surrounding them. Accordingly, I've wondered if the tension and commentary of an unfortunate birthing process threaded two nagging forces within me. The first, an insecurity about my appearance, drove me toward introspection. The second, a highly developed survivor's spirit, prompted me to overachieve.

Through the years these practices of introspection and achievement became so enmeshed I didn't know which was the cause or the effect. I did know, however, that my parents loved me intensely. After I surprised the doctors by reaching five pounds and going home, my mother and I outdid ourselves fattening up my bones. I have the smiling, chubby childhood photos to prove it. I'm sure I enjoyed every bite of the attention, but as I grew up, mirrors and photos eventually caught up with me. When Mother looked at her youngest and last child, she saw a sweet cherub. When I looked, I saw a fat girl.

Out in the World

If I could have stayed in my family's womb, with its propensity toward weight gain, my size wouldn't have been an issue. But too soon children forge their way into a world of comparisons and judgments, and even if the remarks about one's appearance don't intend harm, they still hurt. Interestingly, it's the comments and actions from adults in my childhood, not my friends or classmates, that stuck with me.

At a church potluck dinner a woman approached me from behind, patted my shoulders and laughed, "You certainly are a *solid* little girl, aren't you?" It didn't help that she was the mother of a boy I secretly admired and I immediately felt ashamed. I endured repeated "chunky" assessments at church, but the nurse's office ranked as the most-dreaded place of my grade-school years. Without a thought for our feelings she lined up the class and weighed us one by one. I could have survived this without embarrassment, but the nurse proclaimed each child's weight *out loud*, to be recorded by an assistant across the room. I wanted to be the last one in line and therefore the only child in the office when she weighed me, but we filed in alphabetically and since my surname began with a "C," plenty of children could hear my weight and snicker.

I weighed more than most of my classmates, but the extra insulation didn't shield my sensitive soul from the pain. I felt different, ugly, alone. Somehow I decided my thighs were the fattest of all, and wearing shorts, slacks, or a swimsuit in public traumatized me. I constantly wanted to hide my legs. If she'd known, my mother would have tried to relieve the agony but it burrowed so deep within, I couldn't express it. Even now, as she reads these pages for the first time, my confessions will surprise Mom. She would have wanted me to tell her. I wish I'd told her too, because my struggle deepened in the years to come.

Looking at My Looks

In junior high the word "popular" dominated my thoughts. The popular girls, mostly cheerleaders and their elite friends, gathered each morning before classes in "the hub," a small glassed-in conference room across from the principal's office. The popular girls giggled together and flirted with the equally popular boys, providing a show for others to watch and envy. Most of all, the popular girls were slim and pretty.

I was not a popular girl. By this time I wore glasses and pimples, and teachers pegged me as a shy student. Aware of my weight and other imperfections, my tongue tied in the presence of popular and extroverted peers. In the mornings I slinked by the hub, glanced quickly at the girls lingering there, and hurried to my locker. I wanted, *really wanted*, to bounce into that glass room and chat, but the probability of rejection ran too high. I couldn't afford the humiliation. Instead, I dove deeper within myself. At night I fantasized about being petite and flawless, witty and well-dressed, athletic and sought after. But in the morning the mirror told me differently.

Today I believe this youthful preoccupation with my looks underscores a negative power of the peer group and our culture's outrageous emphasis on bodily perfection. But who would think that at age fourteen? I only knew being out in the world felt unsafe because I didn't look alluring. On the other hand, I was well loved at home, where we seldom talked about appearance. There I learned about a relationship with the Creator, doing the best I could with my talents, and that parental love would last for a lifetime, no matter what. I don't know if psychologists would agree, but I believe this acceptance and a reverence for God's commandments kept me from becoming anorexic, bulimic, or promiscuous to compensate for feelings about my physical self. However, at this stage I didn't know how to let these influences heal the pain.

So I turned to dieting. One summer I ate a thousand calories daily and exercised one to two hours each morning. I lost twenty pounds and it felt wonderful for awhile, as if someone had handed me a new power. But I found other things to worry about: my skin, my hair, my clothes, my glasses. The weight loss didn't make me popular, either. I was still shy at school and within a year I gained back more weight than I had lost. I entered high school feeling frumpy and insecure, and waded through those days trying to avoid mirrors.

As a sophomore I transferred to a school where I only knew two other students. Adults may consider a new school a "fresh start," but most adolescent minds don't think that way. Or at least mine didn't. Even though I wanted to attend this college prep high school, the change didn't alleviate the anxiety of needing to acquire new friends, and my appearance anxieties ballooned. Once again I felt unacceptable, and I spent my lunch hours in a girls' restroom. I was too afraid to venture into the cafeteria and sit alone among students whom I thought looked better, seemed happier, and clustered into impenetrable subgroups. I don't remember much else from those nine months, except that on the bus rides home I often felt depressed.

Somewhere in the next two years I decided if I couldn't make a mark with my looks, I would excel elsewhere. My survivor's spirit kicked in. I joined the school's choir and a small vocal group, participated in the annual musicals and landed a position on the newspaper staff. I earned a listing on the honor roll and took private voice lessons. Music especially gave me a place to belong and hide: choir kids bonded together through long rehearsals and weekend performances. I even had a boyfriend in my senior year.

Looking back, I marvel that I managed these involvements. Musical tryouts, performing for audiences, and scholastic competitions tied my stomach in knots and I shook while enduring them. I think my desire to feel acceptable loomed so large, I'd do anything to achieve in activities that didn't depend on my face, figure, or popularity.

And the boyfriend? I remember never feeling pretty enough for him, even though he professed love and complimented my appearance.

The Omnipresent Obsession

Perhaps in my growing-up years it would have helped to know I wasn't alone in worrying about my looks.

Perhaps it wouldn't have helped me at all. An appearance obsession has permeated our culture for so long, we've internalized the quest to look good—or at least the *desire* to look good—as part of our personal psyche. Someone else's struggle doesn't alleviate our own; we each carry an individualized burden.

Although body acceptance comprises all parts of our anatomy, most of the formal research on women and appearance uncovers a preoccupation with weight. According to body-image experts, the fear of fat is reaching neurotic proportions. Judith Rodin, Ph.D., who specializes in body-image issues, explains, "People today are far more critical of themselves for not attaining the right weight and look. Body preoccupation has become a societal mania. We've become a nation of appearance junkies and fitness zealots, pioneers driven to think, talk, strategize, and worry about our bodies with the same fanatical devotion we applied to putting a man on the moon. Abroad, we strive for global peace. At home, we have declared war on our bodies."[1]

This war has escalated in the last two decades. Females are significantly more disgruntled with their looks today than in the 1970s when I finished high school. Assorted research studies claim anywhere from 48-90 percent of us are concerned or unhappy about our appearance and/or weight, and at least 50-60 percent of women with a healthy body weight think they are fat.[2] In one study of 33,000 women, almost half said they'd rather lose 10-15 pounds than achieve success in work or love.[3] Accordingly, seven out of ten dieters only want to maintain their weight or lose up to ten pounds.[4] We feel so afraid of weight gain, we just keep dieting, even when most doctors would say we don't need to.

Teenagers and twentysomethings suffer the most in this battle, although females of all ages are affected. Recently, after compiling the results of a survey on body image, the editors of Mademoiselle magazine told readers: "When we talked to 500 women, aged 18 to 30, we discovered that although many of you do seem to have pretty decent relationships with your bodies, there's also plenty of evidence that your self-image is just plain lousy. How do you love/hate yourselves? Let us count the ways." While 88 percent of the respondents said they liked their bodies, they still used words like *fat, thick, chubby*, and *overweight* to describe themselves.[5] The young women answered a body-contentment question according to what they wanted to say (they liked their bodies) rather than how they actually felt (they hated their bodies), and researchers caught them in the act.

Still, young women aren't the only ones confused about and focused on their bodies. At doctors' offices children as young as eight protest when asked to step on the scales, even though they're normal in height and weight. Preadolescent dieting has increased exponentially in the last decade, especially in older grade-schoolers.[6] In one study 60 percent of sixth-grade girls said they had dieted.[7] By the time they reach junior high, many girls are veterans of the beauty quest, for fear boys and girlfriends will snub them if they aren't thin and good looking.

On the other end of the spectrum, middle-aged and older women try to remove signs of age with diet, cosmetics, exercise, and surgery. "Somehow they have gotten the message that if you do certain things, you should be able to control aging, rather than look and feel your best at whatever age you are," says Ann Kearney-Cooke, Ph.D., director of the Cincinnati Psychotherapy Institute, who also specializes in body image and eating disorders. "Twenty years ago, no one pretended you could control aging. Now, instead of seeing aging as a natural process, these women see it as a defect in themselves."[8]

Even competitive athletes, known for their healthy and muscular builds, feel the pressure to be unusually lean and good looking. "Women who are involved in competitive sports tend to be more critical of their own fluctuations in weight than women who are not active. They see themselves next to other women of similar age and athletic ability. They often feel they don't measure up," comments Judy Mahle Lutter, Ph.D., founder and president of the Melpomene Institute for Women's Health Research in St. Paul.[9] The women we hold up as top specimens of fitness still find fault with their bodies.

An Abnormal Normalcy

Female dissatisfaction with body image is so widespread, it's considered mainstream to disparage ourselves. Yet the struggle with appearance moves far beyond mere nit-picking. "It's now 'normal' for individuals in our society to express concern about their weight and to engage in fitful attempts to change it," says Janet Polivy, Ph.D., professor of psychology and psychiatry at the University of Toronto, who has studied the relationship between self-esteem and weight control.[10] Estimates are that eight million Americans are caught in the throes of an eating disorder, with 90 percent of them female,[11] and the plastic surgery industry has burgeoned, where most clients are women making changes for aesthetic reasons.[12] It's also estimated that by the turn of the century Americans will lavish $77 billion a year on losing weight. As a nation we are prone to spend more on fitness and cosmetics than we do on education or social services.[13]

With the stacks of articles in my office I could continue this litany on lookism, but why bother? In their conclusions researchers agree: Women dislike all or parts of their bodies, particularly their stomachs, hips and thighs. Even without reading the research I would believe this. I'm surrounded by females who look at themselves in the mirror and criticize what they see. In her dance costume my grade-school-aged great niece studies how her thighs appear in leotards. A niece in high school complains about being fat, although she looks cute and shapely. Another niece and her friend, both in their twenties and attractive, visit me for a weekend. Passing their bedroom I hear these young women's self-deprecatory remarks about themselves. An athletic associate in her thirties struggled with her pregnancy because she hated looking fat. My sister in her late forties complains her stomach is too big for her legs. (I've always admired her slim calves and thighs.) A charming friend in her fifties can't stand what aging does to her body. My mother, who just turned seventy-six and looks much younger than her years, thinks she's unattractive. (I think she's lovely.)

Actually, I don't know women who, if they're verbal and honest, aren't unhappy with their appearance in some way. And these are women who have indicated their feelings. I wonder how many of us suffer in silence.

Denying That It Hurts

If the majority of normal-sized women pat their thighs or stomachs and complain, where does that leave those who, according to the dreaded insurance weight charts, *are* actually overweight? Or what about females with balding heads, disfigured faces, or physical disabilities? With missing breasts or bodies riddled by disease? They look at their slim, "normal," healthy sisters and ask privately, *If they think they're ugly, what do people think of me? What hope do I have for acceptance?*

These are understandable and painful questions.

Though some women break through the pain and accept themselves, many more answer these queries by stifling the hurt and escaping within. We participate in a conspiracy of silence, pretending our "unbeautiful" bodies aren't an issue with us; that we live above worrying about such superficial things as diets, cosmetics, and plastic surgery. After all, we have jobs, friends, families, religion, and social commitments. We want others to think well of us, so we embrace a form of denial. That is, if we can't shut off thoughts about our supposedly below-standard looks and deficient bodies, we can at least *act* like it doesn't matter. We think we can fool people into believing we're well adjusted about our appearance, and with time we might even convince ourselves.

Although denial can serve as emotional self-preservation, eventually it betrays us. Our actions belie what our mouths won't speak. We overcompensate by becoming critical and controlling or compliant and clinging; by overspending on clothes and beauty products or neglecting to care for ourselves; by growing materialistic and socially snobbish or withdrawing from and mocking the world; by not attending to what jeopardizes our health or turning into hypochondriacs. Yet people see through the veneer, into our insecurities and addictions, and wish we would be honest and find healing. Or if we can't do that, at least change what bothers us so much.

When we deny unresolved feelings, we repel people with our lack of authenticity. But most of all, we hurt ourselves, as if the inner woman is punishing the outer woman for not meeting a beauty standard. We paste on a smile. Repress parts of our femininity. Squash the emotions. Look the other way. Shut down.

With these attempts to fake it, however, we eventually mirror the obsessed people we're trying not to be. Females with eating disorders experience a blunted awareness of emotions, an inability to label or articulate feelings, and elaborate defense mechanisms.[14] Parallel to them, we can eat three meals a day, snack in between, keep it all down, exercise regularly, maintain an average weight, and apply makeup, but still function as emotional zombies in regard to our appearance.

As anyone might guess, it's really not just the "beauty misfits" and women with eating disorders who court denial. We all can. Granted, most of us practice denial in small, harmless ways. However, when we live with long-term, unresolved issues about our appearance, we increase the potential of living in denial dangerously. Healthy looking on the outside, wasting away on the inside.

Working at Compensations

In college I reverted to introversion until a tragedy shattered my family.

My father died. He, the head of household, the great provider, the problem solver, left us without warning. His heart stopped and mine, barely beating, went numb. Hardly twenty, with a mother who'd never worked outside the home during thirty-some years of marriage, I felt the pressure to "make it" on my own. I thought if I couldn't meet the traditional qualifications for feminine beauty—blond, thin, pretty, social—I didn't stand a chance of marrying soon and living off a husband's income. I'd have to provide for myself. Those brief moments of achievement in high school pointed to a decent brain and a few talents. If I really worked at it, I could succeed in academics and a career. If I couldn't be attractive, I would be smart and accomplished. And that's what I did.

At the time I didn't consciously reason everything this way, but with hindsight I can identify these feelings as one of my underlying motivations for pursuing success. This isn't to say I should have married instead of succeeding. (God has called me to be single and I enjoy it.) Nor does this insinuate that beauty precludes female accomplishment. (I promote women pursuing their talents, purpose, and passion in life. I believe God created every individual to fulfill a unique potential. I am not against women working in the marketplace.) But for years I worked long hours to the detriment of a social life, couldn't feel happy unless I'd been named number one and eventually burned out of energy and enthusiasm. I spun out of control with work, and at the end of a string of titles and awards, I still needed to reckon with my submerged feelings about me.

I'm little comforted by this, but now I know I wasn't alone. Naomi Wolf, author of the controversial and widely read book, *The Beauty Myth*, claims, "Inside the majority of . . . working women, there is a secret 'underlife' poisoning their freedom; infused with the notion of beauty, it is a dark vein of self-hatred, physical obsessions, [and a] terror of aging."[15] Yet we don't have to be women working outside of the home to prove we're in conflict about our physical selves. Women who've chosen a homemaking career are just as susceptible to becoming Super Mom or Number One Volunteer because they feel indadequate.

This tendency also crosses the line of church and state, and Christian women—those who've been taught that beauty exudes from within—can turn into super achievers at church and other ministry activities. We know how to deny our true feelings by substituting them with other things, and for Christians this can translate into spiritual busyness.

It's not that we've all gone crazy. It's that the pressure to look beautiful has grown so pervasive and penetrating, every woman eventually needs to reckon with it. And not many of us know how to diffuse the tension with a realistic grace and balance. Still, if we're willing to face ourselves, we can release the denial and obsession. It begins with understanding the body messages learned from our families.

Chapter Two

ALL IN THE FAMILY

Learning negative body attitudes at home.

My grandmother was a petite woman, the only one in my family. She stole food from other people's plates, and hid the debris of her own meals so that no one would know how much she ate.

My mother was a size 14, like me, all her adult life; we shared clothes. Mother fretted endlessly over food scales, calorie counters, and diet books. She didn't want to quit smoking because she was afraid she would gain weight, and she worried about her weight until she died of cancer five years ago.

Dieting was always in my mother's way, always there in the conversations above my head, the dialogue of stocky women.

—Sallie Tisdale, Former Dieter

For the most part I'm a great cook, but there are some creations I don't master well. For example, fried chicken, baked pies, and sometimes mashed potatoes. A psychotherapist would have a heyday with this confession, for these were favored dishes at the Couchman family reunions while I was growing up.

The first rule for visiting my father's relatives was: Be prepared to eat unabashedly. The Couchmans believed in second and third helpings, nibbling in between meals, too many desserts, and sending everyone home with leftovers. In my mind's eye I can still see my dad and his brothers scattered about the living room, with belts unbuckled and trousers slightly unzipped, sleeping off a hearty meal at my uncle's house. In the kitchen my mom and aunts, still nibbling on leftovers, chatter and clatter while washing the dishes.

The Couchmans grew up working the land, and though only one son actually remained a farmer, all of the siblings' families—fathers, mothers, children— knew how to eat like one. Unfortunately none of us looked like the Grant Wood image of the *American Gothic* farmer holding his pitchfork: lean and lanky with a wife to match. No matter how arduously a Couchman worked at manual labor, he or she still ate enough to maintain the family's trademark stocky build. When together, inevitably a relative would make a self-deprecating remark about inheriting The Couchman Body and we'd chuckle; we knew what that body looked like. For both males and females a Couchman heritage meant living in a short but sturdy frame with a round stomach. (For the men it also meant baldness.) We could laugh because most of us looked "like Couchmans" and we felt safety in numbers.

Underneath the jokes and laughter, though, I sensed pain. Even when my great-grandparents plowed the fields, rotund wasn't admired. I think that fact saddened us all, but we never talked about weight and body image without making a joke of it. Even when Couchmans successfully dieted, they eventually gained back their losses, so the unspoken credo was, "We're stuck with these bodies, so why not enjoy ourselves and eat?"

Once during a visit an aunt turned to my nephew who doesn't carry the Couchman name and apologized, "I'm sorry you had to inherit The Couchman Body."

"That's okay. I've gotten used to it," he replied. And that's what most of us had tried to do.

Fitting into the System

Even with the eating and joking, I didn't fully consider how a family system affects bodies and our attitudes about them until as a young adult I ate a buffet dinner with my friend Cindy and her parents. Moving through the cafeteria line I picked up food items that looked appealing and plopped them on my tray, as anyone in my family would do. When we sat down at the table, with chagrin I realized my tray held twice as many dishes as my dinner companions. I'd always wondered how Cindy's family stayed so slim. Now I knew.

For most of us it takes years before we awaken to how our families affect our body attitudes—and how our experiences are similar to yet different than other family systems. Fitting into my family necessitated keeping the weight up; belonging to Cindy's family focused on keeping the weight down. We may not have realized it then, but we both felt a need to conform to our roots and be accepted.

Cindy used to joke that her slim mother was so disciplined she could eat half a piece of caramel candy as a "treat" and save the other half for later in the day. We'd laugh, but then bemoan that we weren't strong enough to do the same. We were in our late twenties and early thirties, both with decent figures. (I'd lost weight and most of my family was eerily silent about it, as if I'd betrayed the family code.) Not long after, I moved to another state and didn't see Cindy for a few years. Later when she visited my home, she had reduced to true thinness, much like her mother. In contrast, I had gained weight in keeping with my relatives' standard look. Familial attitudes and patterns still wielded powerful influences over us.

According to Judi Hollis, Ph.D., founder of the nation's first eating disorder hospital, when we separate from our families physically, we still can carry their emotional attitudes about food, bodies, and appearance. "A crucial struggle is for parents and children to separate with love," she writes. And if a child carries internal wounds from the parents' messages about her body image, "the relationship of parent and child has to be severed and then slowly soothed and healed into something new. This separation is not just a matter of age or geographics. It is a deep emotional commitment and tie which must be broken for survival to occur."[1]

Contrary to my family's message to be loyal by staying plump, this commitment often involves living up to our parents' standards of perfection regarding appearance.

My Mother, My Mirror

A new mother cradles her infant daughter and coos, "This is my baby girl. Isn't she perfect? Isn't she beautiful?" We may hesitate to agree, but that little matters. She's gazing into the child's face and beaming. We are off the hook, but later we may find the daughter hanging there.

When we arrive on the earth, red-skinned and squalling, our mothers look and see beauty, despite our wrinkled rawness. Along our way to adulthood, though, moms can turn the words *perfect* and *beautiful* into measuring sticks rather than expressions of unconditional love. Mothers can fail to individuate and consider their female offspring reflections of themselves. We become mirrors for their self-esteem. On at least a subconscious level our beauty, intelligence, social savvy, and career achievements mean they're also beautiful, smart, social, and accomplished. Our lack of these attributes mean they lack too.

And so the pressure begins.

Colette Dowling, author of *The Cinderella Complex* and *Perfect Women,* recalls her desire for the perfect daughter. "I had been caught up in the idea of Gabrielle's grandeur in a way that was particularly detrimental, for it had to do with our shared identity as females," she admits. "From the day she was born my inner security had become bound up with having this girl on whom everyone commented so favorably. 'Ah, *bella!*' the Puerto Rican mothers and fathers in our West Side neighborhood would murmur as my blond-haired princess was rolled by in her stroller. *Yes, bella,* I would think, with a small inner smile. Of course, *bella.* Not only *bella,* perfect!"

Colette the proud mother continues her memories of the mirroring daughter. "Who Gabrielle was, how I imagined she was being thought of by others, all the adulation of her especially, fed straight into my own need for enhancement. *What luck,* I thought, *to have this wonderful kid!*" Then Colette the psychologist analyzes herself. "But of course I had no understanding then of what the *concept* of my little girl's grandness was doing for me. Or of how unbearable for her would become my need for her to be extraordinary."

Daughters mirroring their mothers can be obvious, with admonitions to look more feminine, achieve top scholastic grades, become a law partner, or marry a brain surgeon. But often the mirroring is slippery or subconscious. Mothers don't need to express their expectations for daughters to understand and ingest them.

"I never had to tell my daughter to get good marks, or go out and make friends, or exercise herself into a rare specimen of physical fitness," clarifies Dowling. "That Gabrielle's will to excel might have had something to do with my attitude—toward her, toward myself, toward women—had simply never dawned on me."[2] Dawning finally occurred, though, when Gabrielle quit Harvard and spiraled downward in depression and rebellion. Mother and daughter then embarked on years of unraveling their knotty relationship.

We take for granted that an expectation placed on women, and therefore our daughters, is beauty. It is so assumed, so ingrained, that appearance is usually the first attribute mentioned about a female, before her character or endeavors. "You look so pretty!" we exclaim to the toddler. "What does she look like?" a potential suitor asks. "My, you look really good today," say friends when we first meet. "She's great looking *and* smart," comment men at work.

Mothers understand the power of beauty, that it garners attention, but not all moms want the focus on themselves. With true maternal instincts, they want "the best" for their children, including the daughters' appearance. If mothers are beautiful themselves, they want the same adulation for their daughters. If mothers feel unattractive, they hope for daughters with good looks; then perhaps the world will respect their blood creations more than they have been regarded. Maybe the daughters will get along easier in love and life. A fascinating face and body could provide the much-needed edge, beyond the grasp of talent, education, and a congenial personality.

Perhaps. But even well-intentioned expectations can backfire.

Wearing Mother's Mask

For some daughters their mothers' expectations make them feel not thin or beautiful enough. "My mother didn't hold a gun to my head and force me to binge and overeat. No, I did that," says a thirty-four-year-old woman. "But her feelings about food and weight colored my self-esteem and colored my life. In my mother's mind, if you ate 'good food' and were thin, you were a 'good person.' I always felt that any success I achieved was minimized in her eyes because of my weight."

Her mother at age sixty keeps her weight at ninety-five pounds, while the daughter no longer weighs herself. The daughter also recalls her mother's disapproval when she progressed from "average" as a child to "slightly overweight" as a teen to "obese" as an adult. Today the daughter is married to a loving and supportive husband, holds an advanced degree and has a good job, but struggles "in recovery" about food.[3] Her mother's emphasis on body image, whether "rightly" or "wrongly" motivated, still influences her.

Other daughters, whose mothers think them beautiful, can feel the stress to maintain their looks. Joni Johnston, Ph.D., describes the pressure from her mother to keep improving her beauty-contest face and figure. In her book on appearance obsession, Dr. Johnston remembers, "I felt guilty for receiving attention for something that I had done nothing to earn. I was confused that something as random as looks could be given so much emphasis. Perhaps most difficult of all, I felt significant pressure to look as good as I could and to be as nice as I could so that I might somehow feel worthy of all this recognition."[4]

One daughter feels unattractive, the other knows she's attractive but feels guilty. Both suffer from their mother's lack of balance about appearance, wearing a parent's opinions as a mask for their true feelings. Yet an emphasis on beauty, stated or unstated, isn't the only way we don our mothers' masks. We can also take on their denial.

During puberty Maggie wrestled with what she considered her homely face and gangly body. When she mentioned this discontent to her mother, complaining about her hair and features, the reply shot back, "You care too much about how you look. Don't be so conceited!" After several interchanges like this, Maggie understood that in her family the accepted way to deal with feelings of physical inferiority was to ignore them.

Her mother's religious beliefs enforced this idea, claiming that concern about one's appearance was "worldly" and "sinful."

This led to Maggie's belief that to be a "good Christian woman," she should never wear makeup, improve her figure, wear the latest hairstyles, or be concerned about clothes. Into adulthood, she incorrectly perceived God as concerned only with our spiritual selves, ready to chastise those who "fussed" with their physical appearance. She could not comprehend His loving delight in her.

It took years for Maggie, now in her fifties, to discern that religion served as a cover for Mom's insecurity about her own appearance. "My mother didn't like the way she looked, and instead of tackling it straight on and healing her hurt, she submerged it. At our house it was 'bad' to spend time taking care of yourself physically, other than hygiene and some other basics," says Maggie. Yet the daughter understands her mother's pain. "My mom learned this way of coping from her mother, and didn't have the psychological information available to us now," she explains. "If she'd known what I know now, Mom probably would have reacted differently."

What Maggie "knows now" is that to heal and find self-acceptance, we need to unmask distorted images of ourselves, even when the negative influencers are the parents we love.

The Silence of Fathers

While mothers may overemphasize appearance, fathers can fall silent about it.

I've no doubt my father loved his three daughters intensely, but typical of his generation, he almost never expressed those feelings to us. The only time Dad directly complimented my appearance startled me so much I couldn't say thank you. Standing by the front door, about to leave for a photo session to take my high-school senior pictures, my father commented quietly, "You look pretty." Driving by myself to the studio, the tears in my eyes nearly ruined my make-up.

I was the daughter of an emotionally distant father, and true to the psychological profile, I blamed Dad's silence on myself. "Daughters of distant fathers typically grow up feeling inadequate about their looks and themselves, and long to be beautiful while believing they never can be," explains Carolynn Hillman, Ph.D., a psychotherapist who counsels women with appearance issues. "If a distant father likes his daughter's looks, she naturally figures that if only she were prettier, she would get more of the attention she longs for, so she blames herself and her looks for Dad's distance and feels inadequate." If a distant father ignores her appearance, Hillman has observed "she feels even more that the problem is that she isn't attractive enough, and that if only she were prettier he would pay her more attention. Of course, no matter how much she may improve . . . her father doesn't give her the attention she needs."[5]

On the other hand, some fathers distance themselves not because they're too busy or don't want to communicate with their children, but because they feel awkward. When daughters reach puberty, fathers may feel uncomfortable mentioning appearance, for fear of sounding inappropriate as female breasts blossom and hips widen. They may also feel confused. Their little girls have disappeared and these dads don't know how to relate to daughters as young women with a growing sexuality. They may even fear becoming physically attracted to their daughters. At a time when daughters most need their fathers' approval, many men fall silent.

Like many girls I never thought of my father as a sexual being—a full-blooded male—until a college-age incident hinted at his appreciation for the female form. Getting ready to exit the house in my halter top, Mom complained that it revealed too much and demanded that I change my shirt before leaving. We argued back and forth in the living room, then Dad raised his voice from the dining table and said, "Oh, let her go, Opal. She looks good." I couldn't believe my father said that, and I scrambled out the door. (Today if I had a daughter I wouldn't want her outside in that top either.)

In retrospect I wonder if some of Dad's distance during my puberty was his way of respecting and protecting me. Maybe he didn't want to embarrass either one of us. He would have been mortified and revengeful of anyone's indiscretion toward me, especially if it had been his own. My father's rage at some of my sisters' clueless boyfriends displayed his watchdog mentality about his daughters. That anger gave us security, despite the silence.

A Fatherless Nation

More than ever, fathers are silent because they're missing from the family unit altogether. In his book *Fatherless America*, David Blankenhorn observes, "The United States is becoming an increasingly fatherless society. A generation ago, an American child could reasonably expect to grow up with his or her father. Today, an American child can reasonably expect not to. This astonishing fact is reflected in many statistics, but here are the two most important. Tonight, about 40 percent of American children will go to sleep in homes in which their fathers do not live. Before they reach the age of eighteen, more than half of our nation's children are likely to spend at least a significant portion of their childhoods living apart from their fathers."[6]

Although Blankenhorn focuses on cultural movement and the fatherlessness of males, he believes a lack of fathering drives our most urgent social problems, such as crime (including rape), adolescent pregnancy, child sexual abuse, and domestic violence. All of these problems affect women in the culture, particularly women in their homes. Most of these sins create females who feel negative about their bodies. On a less global and simpler scale, absent fathers can't—or at least can't consistently—guide their daughters' sense of well-being about their looks.

With or without fathers in the home, therapists note that when budding females don't receive their fathers' appropriate appreciation of their appearance and womanliness, these daughters can doubt their physical worth for a lifetime. Truly gorgeous women look in the mirror and envision Plain Janes staring back at them. But just as not all mothers talk about appearance, not all fathers remain silent.

Daddy's Little Girl

Parental affirmation is crucial to our socialization, but sometimes it's Dad's communication about appearance that creates our self-doubt. Dr. Hillman, who has witnessed the effects of all types of dads on their daughters, says, "The daughter of the adoring father may well internalize good feelings about her looks from all his adoration, but she typically also strongly internalizes the Beauty Imperative and firmly feels, even though her head may tell her otherwise, that nothing is more important than how she looks."[7] At least on a subconscious level, the daughter fears if her looks diminish, she'll lose favor with her father, especially in her role as "Daddy's little girl."

As an only child, Jane was photographed frequently and dressed up like a princess. "Dad called me his perfect little doll," she says. In a photo taken at age six, Jane appears at an Easter parade with her handsome father escorting her; her mother stands in the background. "My mother always told me how lucky I was to be blond like him instead of dark like her," she recalls. Yet by the time she reached college, being "Daddy's doll" was a burden Jane needed to cast off, but found difficult because of the possible rejection from him.[8]

To avoid misunderstanding, Hillman contrasts the adoring father, who places most of the emphasis on appearance, with the endorsing father, who compliments his child's appearance but appreciates other attributes about her too. The endorsing father doesn't wrap up his ego in a daughter's beauty; the adoring father does. So does the father who complains about a woman's appearance.

A father who criticizes his wife's or daughter's body threads pain into their souls and wields power over them. Putting down a woman's looks can be an attempt to control her, and if her self-esteem is already shaky, the tactic can work. For twenty-seven years Donna has endured her husband's public jokes and jibes about her big nose and ears, so she thinks, *Who else would want me? I must be lucky to have him.* She doesn't consider that her husband needs to change his rude behavior; she blames herself for his discontent. In the meantime, her daughter Brenda, who looks much like her mother, feels she'll never receive her critical father's admiration.

When the father leaves his wife for a better looking woman, he communicates the same message. I have a friend whose husband, after twenty years of marriage, left her for a younger, supposedly prettier woman. He told his soon-to-be ex-wife, "I've always needed a woman with big breasts." Mary looks sexy and attractive, but she has average-sized rather than large breasts. This husband's declaration devastated his wife, and stamped a lasting impression on their small-chested, adolescent daughters. Though Mary has counteracted her husband's attitude with affirming comments to her daughters, she still worries about damage to the girls. "His comments are much more potent than mine," she sighs.

Likewise, fathers who continually comment on other women's bodies can communicate inadequacy to their daughters. If Dad is a habitual admirer of long legs, his short daughter assumes she can't measure up to his standards, nor gain his affection.

Siblings and Other Rivalries

As I lounged on the living room couch one day, my sister Barbara loomed above my teen-aged face and announced, "I see it! There's another pimple popping out on your forehead."

Siblings. When they're good they're really good. When they're bad they damage our self-esteem. Today

Barb loves me and would do anything to help or defend me, but growing up she tackled the job of accentuating my faults. One of the fastest ways to dismantle me was to hurl insults at my appearance, as is the case with most children and adolescents. Yet libelous words aren't uttered just by sisters and brothers; they can spew out from youngsters in the classroom, in the neighborhood, at church, anywhere. It's true that "kids say the weirdest things," but at their worst they're brutal. Sticks and stones may temporarily break our bones, but words hurt us indefinitely.

I only need to scroll through my memory to gather nicknames children christen on one another, names that degrade physical attributes. *Banana Nose, Buffalo Breath, Chicken Legs, Fatty Patty, Four Eyes, Thunder Thighs.* As girls we hear these descriptions, usually repeated *ad nauseam* by foes, friends, and family, and carry these images of ourselves into adulthood. Even when young critics only mean to tease, they stamp lasting impressions on our body image.

At home the teasing and name-calling can ignite through "normal" sibling jealousies and rivalries or in some cases, when parents prefer a good-looking or accomplished child over the supposedly less attractive, less successful children. When we're scoffed at by our siblings or neglected because we're "the homely one," the psychological repercussions sting. "My older sister Betsy was the gorgeous one," says Cheryl. "There was so much attention on her beauty that I got trampled in the stampede toward her. I've spent my life feeling like I never measure up and have coped by disappearing into the background."

The effects of denigrating an imperfect-looking child are obvious to us, but do we also understand the damage of envy against those who possess beauty? Envious onlookers hurl snide remarks, keep them in their place, make them apologize for their appearance. To feel accepted, many beautiful women work at leveling the playing ground by pointing out what is still wrong with them. "I may be thin, but have you noticed my nose?" Or, "My face is okay, but my thighs are enormous!"

A researcher about female relationships tells us, "Beautiful women tell tales of a childhood in which they learned to know their places. They didn't try to shine too brightly (didn't compete) in other areas, such as intellect, sports, leadership; their cup was perceived as already full. 'Who, me, pretty?' the lovely little girl said, denial being the first and most effective defense against envy. If mother didn't communicate the lesson, a sibling did. Sooner rather than later, other girls let the beauty know the wisdom of being 'beautiful but dumb.'"[9] Envy, beginning with family members, keeps these women from developing a healthy view and appreciation of themselves.

It's especially confusing when girls slam into the family's ambivalence about their appearance. Sisters who say "I love you" may also deliver messages of "I hate you because you're pretty." Brothers ridicule sisters because they're taken back by changing, womanly bodies. Mothers who molded daughters into beauties may now envy their children's good looks. Fathers whose egos depend on the attractiveness of women realize their beautiful daughters are prey for men just like them. For the daughters themselves, the family's mixed messages feel confusing and disloyal.

And sometimes that disloyalty shapes into abuse.

The Aftershocks of Abuse

Abusive mothers, fathers, or relatives teach a girl that she and her body are worthless. If a mother can beat and bruise her so readily, if a father can sexually violate her so easily, if she does not matter to them, then she thinks she must not matter to anyone else, not even herself. Usually she believes if she were better or prettier or *something more*, the abuse wouldn't occur, and its aftershocks rumble throughout her life.

Harvard psychiatrist Judith Herman has documented the lingering effects of abused daughters and other trauma survivors, naming shame, doubt, guilt, self-blame, inferiority, helplessness, defilement, and isolation as their primary feelings.[10] All of these feelings can describe how these females view their bodies, and they're especially intense and scarring for those sexually abused through rape or repeated encounters.

"Needless to say, a sexual abuse survivor's relationship with her body and her looks is often filled with tension and unease," adds Dr. Hillman. "Perhaps wrongly believing that her looks brought on the abuse, she may be afraid to look good so she downplays her appearance. If her father (or other abuser) praised her looks while he was abusing her, she may be even more afraid to look good. Some survivors are ashamed of their bodies and are exceedingly modest, though others are not. Still others go to the other extreme and treat their bodies like a barterable commodity."[11] All abuse

survivors need hope and healing, emotionally, rela-
tionally, mentally, physically.

A Common Need for Healing

To some degree most of us need healing from negative family messages about our bodies, regardless of
whether the offense was big or small, intentional or
unintentional, only once or continuously repeated.
Few if any of us were blessed with the perfect family: a
consistently endorsing father, a constantly nurturing
mother, supportive siblings, and admiring relatives
who felt good about their own bodies and passed that
attitude to us. Even if they try not to be, parents, siblings, and relatives are products of our culture. With us,
they live in a time when beauty and physical perfection
have reached the level of idolatry, and body worship is
insatiable about converts.

But take heart. For the sins of the parents, for the
obsessiveness in our souls, for our damaged self-esteem,
there is redemption and freedom in God's healing
hands. To break free, we not only need insight into our
families, but also into our culture.

Chapter Three

THE BEAUTY TRAP

Unmasking the sirens of female perfection.

I made several films about women, but one, my film about a bearded woman, changed my thinking about gender and appearance. In "Keltie's Beard: A Woman's Story," Keltie explains to the camera in one long close-up how she came to the decision to let her facial hair grow, rather than having it removed as the women in her family had always done. She speaks of seeing a billboard in a Toronto subway saying, Get rid of ugly facial hair. You too can be beautiful. "But," Keltie says calmly, "I already knew I was beautiful." She was sixteen at the time.

In the film Keltie speaks of her trip to Africa. Before that trip, she had only and always suffered criticism, abuse, even assault about her beard. "The best I got was silent toleration," she sighs. In Africa, the market women of Kenya considered Katie's beard a tribute to the women of her family, and they honored her accordingly.

I've often wondered how Keltie, a white Canadian woman, had the courage to defy the standards of her own culture so completely.

—Sara Halprin, Professor and Filmmaker

On the cusp of puberty, hidden away and alone in my bedroom, I pored over a slim paperback about looking your best as a woman. I don't remember where I obtained this authoritative presentation about body and beauty. Perhaps my mother handed it to me, much the way she endowed me with a book about sex, and I read it just as heartily.

Halfway through the oversized pamphlet, diagrams helped describe the features of a perfect female face: eyes, brows, nose, cheeks, mouth, chin, neck. Based on this advice I devoted considerable time to inspecting my lips. According to these drawings, on both sides the perfect mouth extended in width to align with the middle of the eye's iris. (Dotted lines on the diagram showed me precisely where the mouth should end.) I measured my mouth and its edges fell short of the ideal. As if that wasn't enough, this beautiful mouth also supported thin lips. My lips looked full and pouty.

My sister Shirley, ten years older and the family's only blond, possessed The Lips. Hers matched the diagram exactly. Though I never talked to her about this aspect of beauty, I wondered how it felt to deserve such a mouth and whether it affected her life for the better. I questioned how two females with the same parents could look so dissimilar. I also knew that whatever I thought or did, I couldn't change the size and shape of my lips.

Reality proved I only needed to wait for the "perfect mouth" to change its standards in the coming years. During my teens the model Twiggy displayed lips like mine and suddenly girls everywhere mimicked their valentine shape. Later when I reached thirty an older woman spontaneously exclaimed to me, "Oh! Some man is going to find your lips very kissable!" By then I'd forgotten about my mouth, but this friend looked at my lips and thought them admirable.

These days I'm intrigued that women painfully inject collagen into their lips to obtain a temporary "fuller look." The mouth I'd agonized over, detailing its shortfalls, is now hip and enviable. Without injections or plastic surgery I own a version of what cosmetologists call "lush Paris lips." Yet even when thin lips smiled at me from the pages of a beauty book, I wondered, *Who decides these things? Perfect face? Perfect eyes? Perfect mouth? Who makes themselves the authority about beauty?*

It all seemed so arbitrary.

And most of the time, it is.

The Land of No Absolutes

There is no person or governing board that determines the ultimate standard for beauty, but our culture lives as though there is. Even with an affirming family unit, we wonder what people "out there" think of our appearance. We check for what the experts say about makeup and clothes. We bemoan that we don't fit the criteria for good looks, whatever that might be at the time. Without realizing it we allow a vague notion of "they" to keep us always comparing, continually guessing, and forever dissatisfied with ourselves. We fall into a beauty trap and can't get out.

We can't escape because these influences are complex and various, shifting in dominance yet saturating us so thoroughly, we forget to question their authority over our self-concept. Or their lack of realism. Instead, we question ourselves.

Karen tells me that as a high school cheerleader she felt obligated to be thin. "To keep my weight down I'd eat only plain spaghetti for dinner and then do lots of leg lifts and other exercises afterwards," she recalls. As a sophomore she kept her five-foot, three-inch frame at 105 pounds, but claims it was excruciating. By her senior year she had increased to a healthy-looking 124 pounds and considered herself "the blimp cheerleader." Even though she looked good at the higher weight, standing next to the other "rail thin" cheerleaders, in front of a crowd that might draw comparisons, she felt fat, ugly, and self-conscious. I'm not sure if anyone commented to Karen about her weight gain, but even without a direct mention she sensed the pressure to conform physically.

As we grow older this pressure can shift, but still, it lingers. "It's like living in a land of no absolutes, but you're still expected to measure up," complains a friend in her forties. "What am I supposed to look like at this age? I feel pressured to look like I did in my twenties, but if I stop and think about it, isn't that terribly unrealistic? How can I look like I did twenty years ago? Everything, I mean everything, gets older and we accept that in cars and houses and appliances, even our pets. But we can't accept that in ourselves. We feel inferior if we don't look like gods and goddesses. Why can't we just look like ourselves and accept that?"

We can, but after understanding how the family unit influenced us, it also helps to identify cultural influencers, the masked and unmasked sirens, who seduce us into unrealistic expectations about bodies and beauty.

A Panic Called Puberty

What woman can forget her plunge into puberty?

Mine occurred after returning home from an out-of-town wedding on Memorial Day weekend and discovered red stains on my underpants. I solved the problem the way twelve-year-old girls do. I yelled for my mother.

Feeling apprehensive, I stood at the top of the basement stairs and asked, "Mom, will you come up here?" Deep in the basement, she was sorting the laundry.

"I'm busy," she called back. "What do you want?"

"Uh, Mom. I need you to come up here."

"But why? Can't you just tell me what you want?"

I descended the stairs and told her. She led me back to the bathroom and unveiled the clandestine world of pads, belts, and pain relievers for cramps. During this session I gathered that my menstrual cycle, as womanly and wonderful as it was, should never be a topic of conversation, except for asking Mom questions while tucked in a back bedroom.

Then there was the exhilaration and embarrassment of my first bra. Again, Mom acted as my conspirator for secretly maneuvering adolescent changes. She ordered the bra, or *brassiere* as she called it, from the Sears catalog. One day it waited for me in a brown paper-wrapped package when I returned home from school.

Mom ushered me into a bedroom and cooing and fumbling, showed me how to snap it on. All size 28AA of it.

That night during supper my father asked the fatal question.

"Opal," he asked my mother, "what did you get in the mail from Sears today?"

"Oh, nothing," she replied, glancing at me sideways with a slight smile.

"Nothing?" Even though he'd begat three daughters (two of them older than me) and should have known better, my father didn't quit. "But I saw a package from Sears."

"Oh, Harold," my mother twittered. "Judy got some *unmentionables* in the mail today." Neither my cotton bra nor my budding breasts ever got mentioned at the dinner table or any place else with the family again.

School, however, posed ongoing problems because of an unwritten, whispered-about tradition. When a fifth- or sixth-grade girl first got a bra, she wore a white cotton blouse without a slip so classmates could detect her new undergarment's shoulder and back straps. It felt torturous if she wore the white blouse and equally torturous if she didn't. Wearing the white blouse showcased our womanhood to the other girls, but it subjected us to giggling boys who, through the tattletale blouse, snapped the back of the bra. I never told my mother this because she considered bras unmentionables. But I felt relieved when, at last, I could wear a white blouse just once and get the agony over with. It convinced me that womanhood wasn't going to be easy to live with.

I confirmed that opinion in junior high when a gym teacher handed me a tiny towel to use in the locker room. Forget about covering my back side; the humiliation centered on which parts of my front side to cover up while traveling to and from the showers. All of my gym class memories funnel to the terror of accidentally displaying my private parts. Except for a few risk takers, most of us turned our bodies toward the wall while dressing or undressing. Bodies were neither seen nor heard, but once in awhile we talked about them. Say, for example, when the gym teacher presented her obscure menstrual cycle talk or while we measured each other for dress sizes in homemaking class.

Bodies showed up on diagrams in science class, but the teacher focused on what dwells *inside* them and who cared about that? We were sprouting hair and breasts, hips and odors, and wanted someone to unravel the mystery for us. We felt confused and embarrassed. Panicked. What was happening to our bodies looked apparent, but talking openly about it, especially with adults, was taboo. So we formed our body outlook from the opinions of one another.

The Power of Peers

Puberty can confuse girls, especially if trusted, older females are reluctant to discuss and help them appreciate their bodily changes. Without guidance young women draw their own conclusions, which can be distorted and damaging to their self-image. A womanly roundness can be misinterpreted as ugly fat; new body fluids can seem unnatural and disgusting; sexual urges can feel surprising and forbidden. Add oily skin, underarm hair, and clumsiness to that scenario, and it's hard for females to love their adolescent bodies. Yet the adolescent years are when we form opinions that carry into adulthood.

"Messages we receive from peers, teachers, parents and other significant people in our lives become especially important in our teens. As our looks change, so do our perceptions. For many of us, the normal self-focus of teenagers turns into a negative preoccupation with our appearance," explains Dr. Johnston. "Adults who believed they were unattractive as teens continue to compare their looks to others as adults. Numerous studies indicate that, because of the intensity of our struggle to achieve a new body image in adolescence, the outcome of this struggle, either positive or negative, travels with us well into adulthood."[1]

As most of us remember, the biggest struggle—and sometimes the greatest power—originates from the peer group. Hanging out with friends, sitting in a classroom or riding on a crammed school bus, a parent's loving affirmations diminish into an echo as we notice who draws admiring attention and who takes the brunt of the jokes. We set our hearts, and often our fluctuating bodies, on looking like the girl who stands out because of her looks, gathering everyone's glances. If this girl is concerned about makeup and thinness, then so is the peer group. If she vomits to lose weight, her friends try it too.

While eating disorders—anorexia, bulimia, compulsive eating—often ignite from family dysfunctions, the peer group's pressure bursts these diseases into flames. In *Reviving Ophelia*, Mary Pipher, Ph.D., alarms us with her accounts of adolescent girls who live in our look-obsessed, "girl-poisoning" culture. After twenty years of counseling young women, Pipher believes they need adults who'll rescue and rehabilitate their lost sense of self. Part of that self has been sacrificed to the pressure of peers and other non-family influencers. Theirs is the pressure to conform, the pressure to be beautiful and thin.

"Because of guilt and shame about their bodies, young women are constantly on the defensive," says Dr. Pipher. "Young women with eating disorders are not all that different from their peers. It's a matter of degree. Almost all adolescent girls feel fat, worry about their weight, diet, and feel guilty when they eat. In fact, the girls with eating disorders are often the girls who have bought the cultural messages about women and attractiveness hook, line, and scales. To conform they are willing to make themselves sick."[2]

Research underscores the reason for this adolescent defensiveness—and that out-of-home influencers extend beyond the usual group of friends to adversaries, acquaintances, teachers, and other adults. By age five, children point to pictures, of thin persons when asked to identify good-looking people.[3] Elementary school children are more negative toward the obese than handicapped children or those from a different race.[4] Teachers overestimate the intelligence and give more attention to thin and/or attractive students, and underestimate and ignore overweight and/or unattractive children.[5] Obese students are less likely to receive scholarships. Most horrifying of all, a recent study found that 11 percent of Americans would abort a fetus if they knew it tended toward obesity.[6] These attitudes may not be expressed directly, but in myriads of indirect ways young girls absorb the idea that "what is beautiful [and thin] is good."[7]

Marion Crook, a nurse who promotes community health, tells young girls, "Teenaged years should be the time we learn about relationships. It should be the time we learn to understand depth of character, ambitions, emotions. When teens spend most of their time, money, and energy on the body beautiful, relationships tend to center around the body beautiful as well. When the teen years are spent 'looking good,' so many of us miss the chance to develop the tools we need to maintain relationships and to judge character."

Crook then predicts the outcome: "Adults who spend their teen years obsessed with their bodies may have trouble judging themselves realistically. They may have missed lying back in the grass, gazing up at the clouds wondering who they were, what they believed in, what mattered in the world to them, where they fit in. And they may be without a dependable, positive body image. . . . No wonder their self-esteem is low."[8]

This undependable body image also affects their relationships with men.

Male Eyes and Egos

Early in their marriage my father warned my slim mother, "If you ever get fat, I'll divorce you." Yet Dad was the first to gain weight—actually, he grew noticeably overweight—and my parents stayed married until the moment he died. Mom only recently related this story to me, probably to shield the young me from thinking negatively about Dad or my own chubbiness. If that was her reasoning, the plan worked. When she told me, the passage of years vanished any emotion about it, although I thought the story's outcome was ironic.

In our daily lives, though, we're vulnerable to what our husbands, boyfriends, and male friends or associates think of our appearance. There is nothing like men's admiration to make us feel beautiful; there is nothing like their criticism to destroy our confidence. When God punished Eve for eating the forbidden fruit He warned her, "Your desire will be for your husband" (Gen. 3:16). For me this explains the womanly penchant toward wanting approval from men; for feeling disgruntled when our "significant other" omits complimenting us. Women longing for men's attention dates back to the first couple's fall from perfection and because humanity brims with sin, we don't always receive the loving male mindfulness we desire.

Despite our longings, staking our self-image on men's opinions sets us on shifting ground. Our culture coaxes males to believe they deserve stunning-looking women and if they haven't matured beyond that myth, their expectations can influence ours. Studies reveal that physical attractiveness affects the frequency of dating for both men and women, but the beauty requirement is stronger for females.[9] Some researchers claim unattractive women are more "neglected" than "rejected," explaining that to be rejected they must first make an impression on men, and many males don't notice these women at all. According to two Harvard professors (both male), "the social neglect they may experience may be psychologically more devastating than active rejection."[10]

Other researchers have observed that what men consider attractive is deemed more valuable than what women think is appealing,[11] and that men frequently put more stock in the opposite sex's appearance than women do.[12] These men's expectations are high and often lethal to women's positive body image.

Once at a restaurant a business associate presented this assessment to me, "Judy, you'd be a real sizzler with your looks if you'd lose some weight." He didn't know I'd recently lost weight and I immediately thought, *Oh, what's the use of trying to look good? It's never good enough!* With age and perspective I've realized he was the one with mixed-up priorities. But at that moment I sat in mortified silence. I thought a man's opinion of me, though misguided and distorted, was more important than my own.

Conversely, women can stereotype and overestimate men's expectations about female appearance, believing they emphasize it more than they actually do.[13] There are men for whom a woman's appearance isn't tied to their egos and when they declare, "You are attractive to me" these males mean it. They love the total woman—mind, spirit, body—but we have difficulty believing it. Too much cultural conditioning or our own insecurities and perfectionism encourage us to believe what we think men think about us.

One researcher elaborates, "I wanted [men] desperately and made the mistake of believing that what they wanted was what women's world demanded: passivity and beauty. Yes, men want the beauty, but they want other things too, such as warmth, kindness, a full heart, humor, initiative. It is women who pin everything on beauty, on achieving whatever degree of it we can, only to disbelieve what we own, never trusting what we see in the mirror. And so, more today than ever, the competition over beauty unto death continues with the judgmental eye remaining other women's."[14] More often than not, we feed this judgmentalism with heaping doses of hype from the fashion and media industries.

Beauty and the Bucks

Last week a cover blurb on a women's magazine caught my eye at the grocery check-out line, so I bought the publication. Leafing through its pages I stopped, dumbstruck, at a fashion layout. A model stood defiantly, legs apart and hands on hips, refusing to acknowledge the reader with her eyes, but it wasn't her stance that disturbed me. The young woman was so thin, she looked like Auschwitz in a Donna Karan unitard. I found nothing beautiful, nothing to emulate, about her gauntness—a skeletal look probably not caused by illness or poverty or heredity, but by a voracious fashion industry that sucks the life out of the image conscious.

In his exposé on the international modeling scene, Michael Gross describes the beauty business as "a factory that feeds on young girls."[15] He's concerned about the physical and psychological damage to models, and rightly so, but the injuries extend far beyond the fashion elite to those in the public eye, such as broadcasters or public speakers, or others in a body-focused profession, such as athletics or health care. Take, for example, female distance runners. "Most women study fashion models for their looks, their style," says Jack Wilmore, Ph.D., professor of kinesiology at the University of Texas at Austin who has examined the eating and weight concerns of athletes. "But women runners also study other women runners, especially those who win races. And what do they see? Skeletons. On runways and awards stands, they see skeletons."[16]

Still, athletes and public figures aren't the only ones watching and mimicking. Thanks to our electronic age most of us are overexposed to the beauty spectacle of hollow cheekbones, flawless facial features, thick and flowing hair, large and firm breasts with thin arms, waists, and hips garbed in clothes that cost two months of a typical salary. The beautiful females portrayed in the media—at the movies, in advertising, on television shows, through newscasts—don't reflect the form and features of an everyday woman.

Seasoned models—the ones no longer afraid to lose work if they speak out—admit to this discrepancy. "I think the image of models is very destructive to women," complains supermodel Beverly Johnson. "A girlfriend of mine recently asked me what to do with her hair. I took a magazine and pointed to a picture of model Christy Turlington with a perfect haircut. I said, 'You see this? This took hours to get. Don't think just because they are models, they wake up looking like this.' One of these days my daughter will be in Vogue magazine, she will weigh 105 pounds and pose in a dress that a 35-year-old woman then will want to buy. That's really unfair. It does a lot of damage to women's self-esteem because it makes them try to reach a goal that they will never reach."[17]

How far is the reach? In inches, the average measurements of a contemporary fashion model are 33-23-33 and the projected size of a Barbie doll, an "ideal" figure familiar to females of all ages, is 36-18-33. The average model is five-foot, nine inches tall and weighs 110 pounds. In contrast, the average American woman is five-foot, four inches tall, weighs 142 pounds, and wears a size twelve. One third of this country's women wear a size sixteen or larger, yet we keep perpetuating the myth of emaciated beauty.[18]

When lighting, camera angles and computer manipulation make these models look picture perfect, it's big bucks for the beauty industry and high anxiety for consumers.[19] According to one industry watcher, today's pretty women are "mannequins with sex appeal, as glamorous as cinema legends, as visible as the designers whose clothes they parade. They earn spectacular loot for their spectacular looks. Because, more than ever, modeling is about money. At a time when spending is down, top mannequins can still make consumers buy, so they are paid millions."[20]

Modeling has become the new Hollywood, though the old tinseltown still contributes its share to the beauty imperative. A popular television sitcom reports that its three female stars wear dress sizes of two, four, and six. A size eight is considered chunky, and recently I watched a television interview with an actress who keeps her dress size at zero. "If I'm up to a size one, I don't feel good," she explained as I waited for a gust of wind to whisk her away. (It didn't. The interview was conducted indoors.) Even the revered Audrey Hepburn didn't display her true form; it was a carefully guarded opinion that she frequently dieted and struggled with "short spells of anorexia."[21]

Screenwriters Stephanie Garman and Holly White tried bucking the trend a few years ago with a script called "Fat Chance." In their movie an aging, overweight star appears on a talk show and declares she's "had it" with dieting and will love herself, fat and all. She inspires millions of women to follow her example. White says nobody purchased the script, even with what would have been a wildly popular ending: One afternoon on a beach, a super-slim sunbather strolls by two chubby women in swimsuits. "Isn't it a shame," says one heavy-set woman to the other, "she has such a pretty face."[22]

And isn't it a shame that emotionally, we can't discern between fantasy and reality? That we feel so pressured by the beauty industry that an estimated 80 percent of us diet and 50 percent are trying to reduce at any given time?[23] That we spend millions on beauty products and fitness regimes, and if these don't work for us, on therapy? Or that instead of confining itself to our personal lives, the media-induced stress of looking attractive seeps into all facets of our existence and accomplishment, including the workplace?

Good-Looking Résumés

When I managed publication departments, it wasn't uncommon for an employee to ask about a potential female hire, "What does she look like?" Even with solid credentials and ample work experience, both men and women wondered about her appearance. Embedded within that question, I sensed the men wanted somebody good-looking to enhance the department's image and to please their own eyes, while the women hoped for a physically unassuming female so her beauty wouldn't prompt them to feel intimidated and competitive. Either way, after a woman's interview at the office at least one employee would comment on her appearance. As a result, I was doubly careful not to hire someone based on looks. I don't consider appearance a major factor in determining a person's work competency, and besides it's immoral, if not illegal, to do so.

Still, the workplace transmits mixed messages about the physical attributes of employees. On one side, laws protect us from being discriminated against or harassed because of our femaleness. On the other side, the pressure for workplace women to look attractive has never been greater. Naomi Wolf of *The Beauty Myth* insists that increasingly in the marketplace, women need to meet a professional beauty qualification (PBQ) to gain or keep their jobs. She claims, "In the 1980s it was evident that as women became more important, beauty too became more important. The closer women came to power, the more physical self-consciousness and sacrifice are asked of them. 'Beauty' becomes the condition for a woman to take the next step. You are now too rich. Therefore, you cannot be too thin."[24]

Wolf cites a truckload of research to back up her premise. And whether or not we agree with her, we can concur that judicial decisions about women's appearance at work have complicated the issue. In the case of *Craft vs. Metromedia, Inc.*, a judge supported firing a female newscaster because she was "too old" and "too unattractive." In *Hopkins vs. Price-Waterhouse*, a woman was denied a partnership because she needed to "walk more femininely, talk more femininely, dress more femininely, and wear makeup." In the British case of *Jeremiah vs. Ministry of Defense*, employers didn't appoint women to higher-paying jobs because the work was dirty and it might destroy their appearance. In his ruling Lord Denning explained, "A woman's hair is her crowning glory . . . She does not like it disturbed, especially when she has just had a 'hair-do.'" The employer's counsel argued that asking women to ruin their hairdos would lead to industrial unrest.[25]

According to Wolf, women in the workplace—and consequently women in the courtroom—are in trouble if they're not attractive enough. However, most frequently the pressure to look good is subtler than a judge declaring that women experiencing Bad Hair Days are dangerous. The PBQ creeps into the hiring, competing, promoting, and relating inherent in our jobs, in ways that can be difficult to pinpoint and are cumulative rather than isolated in effect. Penetrating looks, targeted jokes, comments on evaluations, subtle put-downs, too little attention from coworkers, male or female, can keep us ill at ease about our appearance. *Do we look good enough to be appreciated? And what do people really say about our looks, our imperfections, when they're behind closed office doors or in restrooms without us?* We may ask these questions as we look into the mirror, knowing that people—even the best of them—can take potshots at us.

Yet not looking good enough is only half of the workplace dilemma for women. Wolf and other experts believe that in certain situations, beauty hinders women's success in the marketplace. A growing body of literature reveals that attractiveness enhances women's success at work only until they aspire to managerial positions. Then good looks turn detrimental because there is a reluctance to accept attractive managerial women as competent.[26] Unfortunately, this rings true in churches and Christian organizations, as well as in the secular workplace. Both male and female coworkers may ask, *How did she get that job?* Or they add, *In what ways did she use her looks and feminine wiles to charm the men who hold the power?* It stings to work hard to reach a level of competency and influence, then be considered the "token woman" or an "airhead" when a treasured job finally becomes ours.

If women choose the work of homemaking, the same erroneous assumptions may be applied to them. If homemakers are good looking and especially if they're blessed with possessions, it's assumed beauty captured the men who gave them homes and now support them financially. Never mind that they work hard keeping up their houses, raising their children, and sacrificing for and contributing to their husbands' work. If homemakers are not attractive, then critics might assume they "can't make it in the outside world," particularly in the workplace.

No doubt, there are women whose beauty garnered them jobs and entitlements they don't deserve, but there are many more who have worked diligently and honestly for advancement. And in most cases, incompetence eventually reaps its own reward. A friend once told me about her workplace, "The women go up really fast around here, but if they can't handle their jobs, they come down fast too." Hopefully, we'll reach a time when all employees are judged by their competency, but we aren't there yet. In the meantime, it's distressing for female managers to encounter the prejudice of "She's so good looking, she must have had some extra help getting that job." Or, "She's so ugly, she must be competent." In regard to work, many women still stand between the metaphorical rock and a hard place, and this location can crush a sense of well being.

Living with Chronic Disabilities

Several years ago my back dislocated while sitting in an airplane seat and when I tried standing up at the flight's destination, pain bolted through me. As best I could shuffle through the aisle, bent at the waist, with tears tricking down my face. I'd waited for the other passengers to leave before hobbling out, but by the time I reached the exit door a line of flight attendants stood behind me and a descending set of stairs appeared ahead. As I painfully touched each step, I heard the groans and complaints of the airline personnel following me. There were no offers to help, no words of sympathy, only the whispered disgust of being slowed down by a woman whose body had betrayed her.

This is how it feels to live as a disabled person, I thought as I ascended another flight of stairs to the terminal, alone and crying.

Despite bed rest, chiropractic care, and pain pills, for weeks I walked stooped over. In this condition at a grocery store I asked a young clerk about a product. She talked to me loudly and in oversimplified terms, as if I might not understand her. After she left I realized, *She thinks I'm mentally disabled! Just because my body is bent, she thinks my brain is too!* I wanted to find her again and pontificate about my master's degree and published books, but it would have taken too much energy.

During that same store visit an acquaintance spotted me and turned away, as if she didn't know what to say. Even after I returned to work an employee sniffed, "I've seen back problems, but nobody who's had to walk like that!" Her comment suggested that perhaps I was faking it; no one could feel that poorly from a back injury.

I wanted to go home and stay there until my body fully recovered, escaping a world that fears and disdains affliction.

But what about those who can't recover? The physically and mentally disabled? The scarred and diseased? Those who've lost limbs and organs, functions and mobility? How do they feel about their bodies? Or how does our culture make them feel? Within the reams of published works about women and body image, little emerges about the physically disabled. Our society virtually lives and publishes as though they don't exist. Are we afraid "it" could happen to us? Will their struggles make our grievances look petty? Are our body prejudices so insipid that we can't look and relate? Perhaps all of these unenlightened questions nag at the core of a culture that seeks physical perfection.

As with women in the workplace, disabled females can face polarized opinions about their abilities, based on their appearance. "Most non-disabled people cannot wrap their minds around the possibility that someone can be disabled or ill and also work productively, have intimate relationships, or be happy," comments Susan Wendell, who suffers from Chronic Fatigue Syndrome. "People without disabilities tend to assume that a person with a disability is unable to participate in most of the life activities they consider important. Thus they infer that someone who can work at all cannot be significantly disabled. Overcoming the common assumptions about disability is a long-term project in which I have found many brilliant women and men engaged. Their struggle is now my struggle."[27]

Whether the struggle is with a disability since birth, an accidental impairment or a physical change from surgery, the need to accept one's "different" body is acute. "People quickly look at my chest and then look away, saying nothing to me," says a woman with a recent mastectomy. "They're trying to find the missing breast, but they don't want to talk about it either. It makes me feel like a freak."

When ill or disabled women get past their own negative feelings, they still encounter the stares and misunderstandings of others, so the road to inner peace can be long. Interestingly, when disabled people are celebrities or unusually gifted, our culture applauds them. We respect the Barbara Jordans and Joni Tadas of the world—the ones in the spotlight for their accomplishments—but for the most part, our culture's messages about beauty and perfection make it difficult for the disabled to feel accepted by others, even when they appreciate themselves.

The Pain of Pornography

There is a disability that robs women of respect for their bodies: a disease of the soul called pornography. I used to think pornography confined itself to peep shows and skin magazines purchased by identifiable derelicts, but today it permeates our culture so thoroughly, porn is acceptable in "normal" households and "read" by people we'd least suspect as abusers. Increasingly, we're accommodating the practice of turning bodies into marketable products for objectification, particularly female bodies.

Several situations opened my eyes to the everyday acceptance of pornography. When photographers and filmmakers want women to strip to the skin for their magazines and movies, there is no shortage of females to participate, and it's not the stereotypical "sleazy" ones who sign up. Pop singers, movie stars, aspiring models, and everyday moms and office workers are willing to bare it all.

"There are two kinds of women," insists a photographer of nude women, "those who pose for *Playboy* [magazine] and those who wish they could."[28] His is a brash and false statement, but he does represent the growing opinion that "showing it all" to a leering world is praiseworthy rather than shameful, even if the exposure is meant to be degrading. Too often these women don't consider the regret and many avenues of pain they can travel by devaluing their bodies this way.

"Posing in the altogether is a risky business," explains one observer who has listened to women's stories about nudity in front of the camera. "Women who try it are tightrope walking between using the session for their own ends and being used to take in money for the sex industry. There have been some disastrous falls."[29] These disasters have included public humiliation, marriage break-ups, various addictions, gratuitous sex, rape and beatings, even murder.

In addition, it seems women are more frequently participating as voyeurs with pornography, by themselves or with sex partners. Instead of complaining about the degradation of women through porn, mainstream women's magazines now publish articles about "Why I Pose for Pornography" or "How a Little Porn Goes a Long Way in My Love Life." Women discuss the differences between "bad porn" and "good porn," and how the "good" skin flicks enhance their sexuality. Even a columnist who dislikes pornography admits, "I'm not going to get hysterical if my lover occasionally picks up a skin magazine or tells me he wants to rent an X-rated video,"[30] missing the point that addiction begins with one act.

Closer to where I live, though, has been the discovery by friends that their husbands (who are now their ex-husbands) read and watched pornography. These men kept it a secret from their wives for years, though one wife explained, "I always knew something wasn't right in our relationship, but I couldn't figure out what it was. I often felt he wasn't attracted to me." The other woman said, "When I found out, I felt used by my own husband. If he could objectify these women, I probably didn't mean much to him either." Both women feel what they looked like wasn't enough to please their men, and that it will take years to recover a positive body image.

The Inevitability of Aging

In all of our encounters with the culture's body mania—the media, the workplace, our relationships—we can't avoid the eventuality that aging foils our wish for flawless beauty. Yet while age and its physical changes are inevitable, many still hope to banish its marks on faces and bodies. Younger women tend toward denial, thinking, *It won't happen to me.* Older women running out of youthful looks spend time seeking potions and methods to turn back the clock. To some degree all of us hear the eternal timepiece ticking, and like my friend who turned fifty and received a solicitation from a retirement magazine, we exclaim, "Not me! Not yet!"

Aging reminds us that our days on earth are numbered. Aging alters how we understand ourselves and how others perceive us. And though unfair, looking older can affect our employment and relationships, our contentment and aspirations, if we don't win over the myth that only young is beautiful. If we don't love ourselves and through our comfortableness, prompt others to accept us too.

In movies and magazines, we're supposed to be encouraged by actors and models in their forties, fifties, and sixties who still look beautiful; but if we listen carefully, the message is, "We still look young, don't we? Rather than, "We are growing older gracefully," or "Aren't our wrinkles beautiful?" We can also remind ourselves of the time, money and assistance required for these women to look so fabulous. "It's their job to look beautiful," says a friend who earns a living sitting at a computer. "I could look gorgeous, too, if I had lots of time and money!" What she means is, "Why can't my aging be acceptable?" Why can't sags and wrinkles, gray hair and weight gain be wise and wonderful?

"In earlier times I would long ago have been urged to loosen up my corsets and hang up my spurs, assuming I were still alive to do so," claims a thirty-six-year-old poet. "Not today. Today I am urged on every side to fight the encroaching decay of my person. I should slather my face with makeup by day and collagen cream by night. I should take up running or aerobic dancing and resign myself to 1,200 calories a day for life. I should dye my hair. Women's magazines treat beauty care and dieting as a female moral duty: rich foods are 'sinful,' failure to exercise is laziness. I did dye my hair once, and it did indeed look browner. But basically, I don't want to do any of these. In fact, I resent very deeply the suggestion that I should. Does this mean I accept age gracefully? No, actually, I'm furious."[31]

At least on bad days, many females pass through this valley of anger before learning to live peaceably with the physical aspects of maturity.

Our Unhappy Metaphor

With the culture hammering at us to scrutinize, beautify, and display our bodies, with the physical realities of age, stress, illness, and birth-endowed features, it's easy to bounce between two polar views: to believe we need to relentlessly pursue attractiveness or to feel we're so hopeless, we're not worthy of any attention. Yet to accept one of these "solutions" robs us of our God-intended celebration of who we are, of living fully, with satisfaction.

Still, in our culture, in our hearts, we are ripe for change. Those who've relentlessly pursued beauty are noticing the emptiness of that search. Author Nancy Friday writes, "For ten years—and the clock is still ticking—we have been living in the belly of beauty, focusing on it as never before in my lifetime, and deriving little pleasure from it, I might add. Nothing satisfies, nothing endures; we go through fashion statements as we go through love affairs and marriages. Beauty is the allegory by which we remember these years, a metaphor we will later ponder, asking, why was no one happy then? Whatever we may buy to please ourselves—cars, houses, vacations—we buy beauty with more desperation, investing in its power because of the gnawing envy we feel when we see beauty in others."[32]

So how do we wrest away from the desperation? How do we transition from body mania into a nurturing, reasonable acceptance of our appearance? The answer lies in applying spiritual truths to our physical existence.

Chapter Four

REFLECTIONS OF EVE

Understanding the Creator's view of us.

My experience with women of size in Mexico caused me to question the entire set of analytic premises about women's various sizes and shapes and especially weights. An old psychological premise in particular seemed grossly erroneous: the idea that all women of size are hungry for something; that "inside them is a thin person screaming to get out."

When I suggested this "screaming thin woman" metaphor to one of the majestic Tehuana tribeswomen, she peered at me somewhat alarmed. Did I mean possession by an evil spirit? "Who would have put such an evil thing inside a woman?" she asked. It was beyond her comprehension that a woman would be considered by "healers" or anyone else to have a screaming woman within because she was naturally big.

—Clarissa Pinkola Estés, Psychotherapist

In the dimly lit classroom my art history professor, with a click of the slide projector, casts an image on the screen before us. He is discussing Paul Gauguin's Post-Impressionist artwork. Usually I feverishly scrawl notes across legal pad pages, but for several moments his voice fades into the background as I examine the intriguing painting—a simple portrayal of a Caucasian woman mending her dress.

Hmmmm, what is that underneath her arm? I ask myself. *A pillow? Another item for mending?* I squint at the screen and then identify it. It's her stomach. A flabby, stick-out-for-inches abdomen. Gauguin has painted a woman with an imperfect body. *Good for him,* I think. *And kudos to the woman for letting him show her that way.*

Actually, I shouldn't be surprised by the protruding stomach. My abdomen is out of shape, so it's not as if I haven't seen one before. I also know that Impressionist and Post-Impressionist artists, midst a torrent of controversy, insisted on depicting flawed rather than idealized women. During the nineteenth century, France's artistic salons primarily dictated what constituted "good art." And part of the criteria was to paint or sculpt upper-crust or mythological women with porcelain skin and perfectly contoured bodies. In contrast, certain Impressionist and Post-Impressionist artists endowed some women with uneven skin, wide arms, sizable stomachs, and dimpled thighs. These were everyday women from middle and lower classes: real women looking like themselves, cellulite and all.

Today these "radical" artists—particularly Degas, Monet and Renoir—are beloved by the masses, yet most of their female creations couldn't pass an end-of-the-twentieth-century beauty test. Neither could women painted by earlier, celebrated artists like Boticelli, Michelangelo, Rubens, or Rembrandt. Our culture would judge these women too fat, irregularly shaped, not feminine enough, or all of the above.

Recently while leafing through a book about the restoration of the Sistine Chapel, I was struck by the thick, muscular build Michelangelo assigned to Eve in the great fresco's representations of her. In all three depictions of the first woman—the creation, the temptation, the fall—she has substantial arms and thighs, plus a bulging stomach. Yet Michelangelo's muscular Eve, Boticelli's pot-bellied damsels, and Renoir's plump models were considered beautiful in their day. It is our era that feels uneasy with the natural roundness of the female form, whittling it away into nothingness.

Even so, we aren't the first people to devise our own, if not peculiar, definition of feminine beauty. Since Eve emerged from Adam's rib, cultures have been throwing the female figure on an ever-whirling potter's wheel, remolding and recasting her shape again and again, ever changing the criteria for female perfection, never satisfied with how the original Creator intended her to look.

Changing Times, Changing Beauty

In the twentieth century alone, the West has swayed back and forth in its perception of ideal beauty. At the turn of the century women padded themselves and wore bustles to ensure a mature appearance. Twenty years later during the Jazz Age, the preferred shape looked boyish, with no waistline and cropped hair. Curves returned in the 1950s when Marilyn Monroe led the way with full breasts, hips, and thighs, yet a cinched-in waist. By the 1970s the Earth Mother image and loose clothing "let it all hang out," but not for long. The 1980s punished her magnanimity with its gladiatorial approach to figure development: women needed to be fit and strong with no body fat.[1] At the end of the century the fitness criteria remains, although we're also to look gaunt.

Several months ago, after re-watching Barbra Streisand in the movie *Funny Girl*, I remarked to a friend, "I was surprised. Barbra looked sort of plump in that movie. Not at all what she looks like now."

"That's what women *looked like* back then," my friend countered with an intensity that revealed her frustration with the "thin is best" mentality. "It was *okay* for her to have some fat." I conceded, but realized "back then" was barely thirty years ago. Compared to how long people have inhabited the earth, our idea of physical beauty alters quickly. In one lifetime, to keep up with what's deemed beautiful, our culture requires women to expand, contract, and contort their bodies repeatedly.

Paging through history, we discover societies with widely varying paragons and pursuits of beauty. Some have accepted the design inherited from their ancestors; others have religiously tried to defy nature. However, it appears every culture has defined female beauty in a way that keeps women concerned about some aspect of their appearance. Reaching their culture's physical ideal has meant social acceptance, and the outcome has ranged from the interesting to the terrifying. Consider the following examples.

Around 2600, B.C., in Mesopotamia, Sumerian women wore loose, flowing dresses, so body size wasn't an issue. Their weight could fluctuate up and down, and probably wasn't noticed much. However, this placed great emphasis on what protruded from the body-disguising gowns: the face, hair, hands, and feet. Ideal Sumerians wore elaborate hairdos and lavished time on manicures, pedicures, and makeup. Later, in 1400 B.C. Egypt, wide shoulders with narrow hips on both men and women gathered admiration. Surviving Egyptian drawings and paintings don't deviate from this pattern, although it's difficult to believe many achieved the extreme ideal of an inverted triangular torso. Only foreigners were portrayed as fat.

In the Middle Ages, women who fasted themselves into an anorexic condition were considered pious and close to God. In contrast, seventeenth-century England respected overweight people because only the wealthy could afford enough food to grow fat. French women before the revolution looked pink and plump. They weren't limited to one size or shape but were judged by their clothes, and the more elaborate and cumbersome, the better. Wide skirts stymied the acts of sitting down, passing through doorways or walking on the street. The quest for beauty even claimed the lives of some women: if gowns caught fire, they couldn't escape with their lives; if they fell from boats, the heavy skirts sank and drowned them.

Dieting appeared in America during the 1830s, under the guise of a new morality called wholesome-ness. Though diet experts emphasized healthy living, the playbills, fashion plates, and literature lauded slender women. It didn't take long for thin to be "in."

The advent of life insurance studies in the late nineteenth century intensified the desire for thinness by frightening women into unrealistic expectations about their bodies. A health practitioner explains, "Their studies did not accept average weight as a natural weight. Instead, they picked a low-weight ideal, wrongly implying a low weight would prevent death. Anything more than "ideal" was considered overweight. They picked out these studies on men and applied them to women, creating an amazing chart of inaccurate, inapplicable, impractical, and dangerously misleading information that influenced the public for decades."[2]

As expected, these weight charts encouraged people to purchase life insurance because they felt vulnerable to death at an early age. A major life insurance company reinforced this idea in the 1940s with its widely accepted height/weight charts that made most people appear overweight, and we still haven't recovered from our fear of fat.

However, while some of these quests for beauty pushed the edge of reason, they didn't attempt to alter the basic structure of women's bodies. Tragically, there are other cultures whose attempts at shaping the female figure and thus, defining beauty, have plunged women into chronic pain by altering their God-endowed skeletal form or eliminating body parts.

The ancient Chinese ritual of foot binding ruthlessly insisted on stopping the growth of women's feet. Women with small feet were the essence of desirability, but as a result of the binding, soles sloughed away while the toes broke and bent backwards. Sometimes one or more toes dropped off, and women with exceptionally small feet, due to bent or missing digits, were carried from place to place. Though admired as beauties, they could no longer walk on their own. Still, women endured the pain and humiliation. If females were called "large footed demons," they bore the deeper shame of never marrying.[3]

The Mayan Indians of Central American and several Native American tribes bound their babies' heads with boards to produce long, flattened skulls, which they considered beautiful. Some Victorian women surgically removed one or more ribs to achieve the coveted hour-glass figure. In Burma the Paduang tribe still attaches rows of metal rings around young girls' necks, adding more rings as they grow toward adulthood. The rings depress shoulders and elongate necks, rendering women unable to support their heads without them.[4] Muslin girls in West Africa can't marry unless they endure genital mutilation. In this procedure, also intended to keep females from sexual pleasure, "women excise the clitoris with unsterilized broken bottles or rusty knives, leading often to hemorrhage and infection, sometimes to death."[5]

And all in the name of beauty.

Knowing the Spiritual Truth

The ancient Scriptures speak of people who are "ever learning, and never able to come to the knowledge of the truth" (2 Tim. 3:7). In essence this is the futile path women have trod in their ceaseless quest for beauty, flogging themselves all of the way. As a culture we are ever changing, ever seeking something we rarely obtain, and never accepting—let alone celebrating—the truth.

The truth is that God, the Master Designer, created each of us as unique and magnificent human beings. The truth is, we're designed to inherit—and can't escape—our ancestors' genetic makeup. The truth is, we're not meant to conform to a culturally enforced standard. We're to be ourselves, and constantly battling our physical composition leads to frustration and spiritual emptiness. An insightful female therapist explains, "Women who are big or small, wide or narrow, short or tall, are most likely to be so simply because they inherited the body configuration of their kin; if not their immediate kin, then those a generation or two back. To malign or judge a woman's inherited physicality is to make generation after generation of anxious and neurotic women. To make destructive and exclusionary remarks about a woman's inherited form, robs her of . . . spiritual treasures."[6]

Sadly, after centuries of pursuing the fleeting and physical, as a culture we've buried our innate need for spiritual treasures under a pile of costumes and cosmetics, diets, and disciplines. We don't recognize and appreciate who God created us to be. Nor do we understand how to discover His true and loving intentions toward us, or to let Him heal our aching souls. Instead, we're searching, even screaming, for what physical eyes can see.

The same psychotherapist who reminds us of our genetic inheritance claims, "It makes utter sense to stay healthy and strong, to be as nourishing to the body as possible. Yet I would have to agree, there is in many women a 'hungry' one inside. But rather than hungry to be a certain size, shape, or height, rather than hungry to fit a stereotype; women are hungry for basic regard from the culture surrounding them. The 'hungry' one inside is longing to be treated respectfully, to be accepted, and in the very least, to be met without stereotyping. If there really is a woman 'screaming to get out' she is screaming for cessation of the disrespectful projections of others onto her body, her face, her age."[7]

On one level this explanation proves true. We would appreciate people respecting our bodies for what they are, and this acceptance would change some of our interactions with the world. But this solution doesn't touch the root of our dilemma. Having other people respect us only paints a veneer on our insecurities. It deals with our appearance anxieties on a physical level when the source of the problem is spiritual. Making peace with our physical selves flows from souls filled with peace. God is the source of true inner peace—a peace that "transcends understanding" (Phil. 4:7)—so to walk away from appearance anxiety, we first step toward the Creator.

Going Back to the Garden

When God created the world and its inhabitants, the biblical account emphasizes that He called it good. Specifically, almost one-fourth of the verses in Genesis 1 end with the declaration, "And God saw that it was good." The Creator found perfection and pleasure in His light, darkness, water, land, vegetation, and crawling, flying, and swimming creatures. Then as a flourishing finale, saving His best work until last, God created the first man and woman. In a final benediction to the chapter, the author claims God called them "very good" (verse 31).

Translated to our culture, the word "good" is a grand understatement. We better understand the significance of God's handiwork by substituting contemporary expressions like "unbelievably perfect," "incredibly awesome," "gloriously magnificent," or "beyond description." In the Old Testament the words for "good" mean "good in the broadest possible sense." The description connotes "the beautiful, the attractive, the useful, the profitable, the desirable, and the morally right."[8] A biblical commentator explains that "creation, fashioned and ordered by God, had no lingering traces of disorder and no dark and threatening forces arrayed against God or man. Even darkness and the deep were given benevolent functions in a world fashioned to bless and sustain life."[9] Such purity almost surpasses our comprehension.

More incredible is the blessing God bestowed on Adam and Eve and their billions of descendants. Genesis recalls, "Then God said, 'Let us make man in our image, in our likeness, and let them rule over the fish of the sea and the birds of the air, over the livestock, over all the earth, and over all creatures that move along the ground.' So God created man in his own image, in the image of God he created him; male and female he created them" (1:26-27).

Created in His image, formed in the likeness of the flawless, holy, loving, compassionate, omniscient, powerful God. Though Scripture doesn't give details about their appearance and personalities, for man and woman to be created in God's image implies they modeled His perfection. Their bodies, minds, and souls exhibited His highest ideal for humanity, for all of creation. Accordingly, Adam and Eve didn't worry about beauty and bodies, even though they lived unclothed before God. And why should they? Every person and thing looked and functioned perfectly, and the couple communicated intimately with the Creator who loved them immeasurably. Stated in today's vernacular, appearance wasn't "an issue." Theirs was a sacred and unself-conscious existence.

The wonderful storyteller Madeleine L'Engle describes the first couple's relationship to God and the new world. "In the Garden of Eden, there was no separation of sacred and secular; separation is one of the triumphs of the devil. All of creation is God's, and therefore it is all sacred. And when everything is sacred, we can understand something about freedom," she explains. "God created Adam [and Eve] in a sacred world in which it was truly possible to be free."[10] Accordingly, God created an environment in which bodies were sacred. Our physicality was not designed to be separated from and "less than" our spirituality; God created it all and said it was good. And if we understand that everything is created by a perfect God and declared good and holy, we're not bent on changing ourselves. We are free to be.

So if God created us as His sacred ideal, if we were designed to live without appearance worries, what went wrong?

The answer lies in a familiar yet often ignored incident.

The Advent of Fallen Bodies

Though God created Adam from the dust and Eve from Adam's rib, He didn't declare exclusive rights to their thinking and decision-making processes. The

Creator infused His people with free will, even though they could choose to reject Him. In my opinion, God eschewed control of their minds because He desired that humans love Him openly and willingly, not from a sense of entrapment or forced obligation. Granting them choice embodied a magnificent act of benevolence—the gift of a secure Father who loved His children unconditionally.

Unfortunately, as earthly fathers tell us, giving children choices doesn't mean they'll make wise decisions. Genesis also unfolds the story of the first couple's predicament, with their fatal choice described in this excerpt:

> The man and his wife were both naked, and they felt no shame.
> Now the serpent [Satan in disguise] was more crafty than any of the wild animals the Lord God had made. He said to the woman, "Did God really say, 'You must not eat from any tree in the garden'?"
> The woman said to the serpent, "We may eat fruit from the trees in the garden, but God did say, 'You must not eat fruit from the tree that is in the middle of the garden, and you must not touch it, or you will die.'"
> "You will not surely die," the serpent said to the woman.
> "For God knows that when you eat of it your eyes will be opened, and you will be like God, knowing good and evil."
> When the woman saw that the fruit of the tree was good for food and pleasing to the

eye, and also desirable for gaining wisdom, she took some and ate it. She also gave some to her husband, who was with her, and he ate it.

Then the eyes of both of them were opened, and they realized they were naked; so they sewed fig leaves together and made coverings for themselves (Genesis 2:25–3:7).

Traditionally this disobedience has been called the fall from grace, the original sin, the death of innocence. And once sin entered into the hearts of humanity, what was the first couple's immediate concern? Not their tarnished relationship with the Creator, but their bodies. What was good and beautiful and perfect suddenly felt inadequate. Adam and Eve filled with shame, despised their nakedness, and clothed themselves. Instead of trusting God with their appearance, they began making changes. By sewing fig leaves together, they abandoned the spiritual and focused on the physical, and the generations have been fussing about their looks ever since.

However, no amount of alteration and beautification has staved off sin's destructive claim on our bodies. Edith Schaeffer, cofounder of L'Abri Fellowship, describes the Fall's devastating results. "If Adam and Eve had not eaten, there would have been no death, no deterioration," she writes. "If they obeyed and respected and believed the Word of God in that commandment, there would have been no abnormality. But they did, and the world, people, animals, all nature have been spoiled, devastated. God's perfect creation has been vandalized and spoiled. Death has come in like a flood spilling out of a dam. Ugliness has blotted out much that was beautiful. None of us has ever seen perfection in nature, in human beings, or in relationships and situations."[11] None of us can reach the physical perfection we secretly desire.

We long for this perfection because the memory of flawlessness—of being made without blemish in His image—is stamped on our souls. We sense that somewhere, somehow, perfection was possible, but the reality of our sin-marked bodies won't allow us to achieve it. This spiritual memory emerges in recent appearance studies. When asked to identify attractive people, research subjects pointed to photographs of individuals with symmetrical faces. These faces look balanced, with features on the left side matching the features on the right side in size and shape.[12] Gravitating toward symmetry hints that we yearn for order and perfection; our spiritual memory remembers what used to be.

However we describe it, we can readily recognize that humanity suffered a physical loss in the Garden. We are not born perfect, nor does our youthful appearance last. Throughout our lives we can implement improvements, even look beautiful for a period of time, but eventually decay catches up with us. Our bodies methodically deteriorate, reminding us of sin's mortality, leading us toward death. Comparing photos of a former Hollywood starlet at ages twenty and eighty uncomfortably reminds us of this fact.

Recognizing our mortality, watching our physical deterioration, we would be doomed to despair, if not for heavenly intervention. Because God's holiness couldn't tolerate sin and because they might eat from the Tree of Life and live with evil's effects forever, God banned Adam and Eve from the Garden (See Gen. 3). Sin cursed man and woman to struggle in their relationships and to toil the earth with sweat and sorrow, but He didn't stop loving and providing for them. The Father was still involved in their lives; the earth was still theirs to subdue.[13] When sin burst on the scene, God set in motion a plan of redemption, not only for their souls, but also for their bodies. Not only for them, but for all of humanity.

Choosing Our Viewpoint

A few nights ago I ate dinner with a group of female friends, most of whom know one another thoroughly and share their opinions openly. At one point the conversation turned to how the recently finished year had served difficulties to us all. Unanimously, we felt grateful to turn the calendar page, hoping that in the coming months life would return to normal, if there is such a thing as normal.

After one woman delivered a litany of her last year's challenges, she said, "I think God is pruning us."

Another friend quickly countered, "I think He's punishing us."

We responded with halted laughter and the conversation rolled on, but later I mulled over the second comment and how often we think of God as punitive instead of redemptive. As I thought about my friend's unsettling remark, I suddenly realized our perception of Him impacts not only our spirituality, but how we face all of life, even how we manage our physicality. If we see God only as a punisher, waiting to trounce on our weaknesses and failures, we stymie our personal and spiritual growth, continually castigating ourselves and feeling worthless.

If we accept Him as the Redeemer, through His forgiveness we can experience freedom, healing and inner sustenance. We can forgive our imperfect bodies and not allow appearance pressures to riddle our self-worth.

Stated in these terms, it seems ludicrous that we would choose anything but a redemptive concept of God, but the Fall's debilitation runs deep and Satan still slithers into minds to distort them. We frequently choose the punitive viewpoint. We get stuck in the Garden, hiding because of our nakedness, terrified to unleash ourselves in the world. Fearful of God.

Nonetheless, the compassionate Father wants to release us from our sin and misconceptions by offering us His most precious possession.

The Holy in Human Flesh

Just as Adam and Eve focused on their bodies after they sinned, God used a physical body for His plan of redemption. He gave us the Holy in human flesh. The Father sent His only Son, Jesus Christ, into the world to dwell among us and share the full scope of life from birth to death. (The Bible says that even today, Jesus sympathizes with our weaknesses because He experienced our physical limitations. See Hebrews 4:16–5:10.) More so, Jesus entered the earth to save humanity from sin, to rescue us from eternal damnation by dying on a cross in our stead. The good news is that Christ didn't stay in the grave, but rose again after three days. He conquered sin and death and returned to heaven, where He prays for us today (Rom. 8:26–27).

Again, because of God's purity He cannot tolerate sin, so without His intervention humanity is condemned to eternal death "for all have sinned and fall short of the glory [the perfection] of God" (Rom. 3:23). But just as one person ushered sin into the world, so a divine individual rescued us from its consequences and offered us eternal life. The gift of salvation is free, available if we repent of sin and accept Christ as our Savior. Forgiveness is ours, just for the asking.

The Apostle Paul elaborated on these truths when he wrote to Roman Christians. Even if we're familiar with God's redemptive plan, we need to sink this explanation deep into our hearts repeatedly.

> You see, at just the right time, when we were still powerless, Christ died for the ungodly.
>
> Very rarely will anyone die for a righteous man, though for a good man someone might possibly dare to die.
>
> But God demonstrates his own love for us in this: While we were still sinners, Christ died for us.
>
> Since we have now been justified by his blood, how much more shall we be saved from God's wrath through him!
>
> For if, when we were God's enemies, we were reconciled to him through the death of his Son, how much more, having been reconciled, shall we be saved through his life!
>
> Not only is this so, but we also rejoice in God through our Lord Jesus Christ, through whom we have now received reconciliation.
>
> For if, by the trespass of the one man, death reigned through that one man, how much more will those who receive God's

abundant provision of grace and of the gift of righteousness reign in life through the one man, Jesus Christ.

Consequently, just as the result of one trespass was condemnation for all men, so also the result of one act of righteousness was justification that brings life for all men.

For just as through the disobedience of the one man the many were made sinners, so also through the obedience of the one man the many will be made righteous.

The law was added so that the trespass might increase. But where sin increased, grace increased all the more, so that, just as sin reigned in death, so also grace might reign through righteousness to bring eternal life through Jesus Christ our Lord (Rom. 5:6–11, 17–21).

The New Testament teaches because of Christ's resurrection and our acceptance of His salvation, the barrier between us and God has disintegrated. Consequently, when God looks at forgiven sinners He sees the redemptive work of His Son. He sees the Son Himself, full of purity and glory. Christ's righteousness is our own; the light of His presence shines within us. In God's eyes we are no longer reflections of Eve and her sin, but the image of Christ's perfection.[14] We are set free—body, soul and spirit—to be who God created us to be.

Redeeming Our Body Concept

So what does God's act of grace have to do with our body concept?

Just about everything.

If we allow the full meaning of this redemption to penetrate our souls, it can transform how we live with our physical selves. We can ignore the world's changing definition of beauty and stand steadfastly in the presence of the One who believes that because of His Son we are "altogether lovely" (Song of Solomon 6:16). [15] Though we live in bodies marked by the Fall, we can adopt a redemptive view of creation, pointing our hearts and minds to God's original premise, agreeing with the psalmist that we are "fearfully and wonderfully made" (Ps. 139:14, KJV). We can declare that because we are fashioned by God, we are beautiful. We can revel in the fact that we bear His image.

In God's kingdom, there are no ugly people. There is no impossible physical standard to reach, only variations on a creative work called humanity. Every person is a unique, one-of-a-kind being. There is no justification for comparing ourselves to one another, for handing out negative judgments about appearance. What the world calls physical flaws and disabilities are not barriers to joy and fulfillment. Disease and illness can be a gateway for conforming us to His image and healing our souls. Aging is not a time to lower our eyes in shame, but a season to lift up hands and celebrate spiritual wisdom and resilience. Death is not the final chapter for our bodies; in heaven they will be transformed and released from sin's influence. [16]

Consequently, when we accept God's revolutionary plan of redemption, we can renew our minds and respond with our own radical step: we can live harmoniously with our appearance. We can make peace with the world's pressure to look perfect.

Chapter Five

MAKING PEACE WITH PRESSURE

Living above negative opinions and judgments.

I was a Christian for almost twenty years before I began determinedly laying down my beauty-related fears and worries. Somehow, my need for spiritual release in this area escaped my attention altogether—even though I constantly worried about my weight, tried to impress people by the way I looked, and was hooked on comparing myself to other women.

When I looked at my [spiritual] sisters, the first things I noticed about them tended to be their size, facial attractiveness, hairstyle, clothes, and jewelry, instead of their personhood. By concentrating on women's appearances, I missed the most important thing: the reflection of God's image in one-of-a-kind style.

—Debra Evans, Author

"But the queen is naked," the little girl whispered to her mother.

Startled, the mother looked at her daughter, then at the queen parading by in front of her subjects. Perhaps the girl was right.

Though she loved the queen dearly, the mother had heard stories about the aging leader's recent obsession with clothes and beauty—about how the queen spent more time fixing her wardrobe and face than reviewing the troops, attending the theater, or fulfilling other royal duties. And how lately two weavers had captured the queen's undivided attention and deep financial pockets with their promise of sewing her splendid garments, unlike any others. According to the weavers, the cloth they created for the queen looked extraordinarily beautiful, but it also held strange powers. It was invisible to anyone who didn't believe the queen still looked young and gorgeous.

Now this greatly appealed to the queen, for she ruled a country that highly valued youth and beauty. In fact, when the former queen showed signs of aging, townspeople stormed the castle and banished her majesty from the kingdom. Though the aging queen ruled her subjects with wisdom and fairness, the people demanded a younger and more beautiful woman be crowned in her place.

During her years as "the younger woman," the current queen reigned without much thought about her looks. But as she grew older, a fearful obsession about beauty gripped her, and she fell prey to the mysterious fabric. *If I owned that cloth, then I'd know which of my councilors were loyal and truthful,* the queen thought. *And I could assure myself that I'm as beautiful as ever.* So she gave the weavers lots of money, fine silk, and gold thread so they could begin creating their masterpiece.

After a while the queen grew curious about the weavers' progress, but avoided visiting their shop, for fear she'd see nothing on the looms and prove her faded beauty. Instead, she commissioned her faithful prime minister to inspect the work and to report on its appearance. By then the townspeople had heard of the cloth's magical powers and also eagerly awaited the results. The prime minister felt the pressure as he ambled to the shop. If so many people believed, he would believe too.

Upon arrival the old prime minister witnessed the weavers furiously at work, but he saw nothing on the looms. Afraid of losing his job, he adjusted his glasses and exclaimed, "What a beautiful cloth! What patterns and colors!" He reported with the same enthusiasm to the queen.

At this point the queen decided she possessed a new way to test her staff's allegiance. She sent a trusted lady-in-waiting to the shop and fearing banishment, the woman also described a magnificent piece of cloth to her majesty. The weavers increased their time at the looms and the number of coins and supplies needed for their task.

Finally the queen visited the shop herself. *Oh, no, it's just as I feared*, she thought while scrutinizing the loom again and again. *I've grown old and ugly. But I don't need to let anyone know*. The queen agreed to have the imaginary cloth cut into a gown, a royal robe and a train—and to wear them at a grand procession through town.

"This material is so light, it feels like a spider's web," said the swindling weavers as the queen pretended to put on her new outfit. Those around her agreed and commented on its great beauty, and how the queen looked stunning. By now the queen felt so much pressure, she swallowed her pride and continued the charade. Two gentlemen of the imperial bedchamber fumbled to pick up the imaginary train as the queen exited the palace to the cheers of a crowd.[1]

The Truth About Lies

The queen was a woman who obviously feared what people thought about her appearance. So much that loyal servants and councilors lied and committed acts of subterfuge on her behalf. So much so, that she surrendered all dignity to be supposedly admired and respected; to be reassured that yes, she was the fairest of them all. So much so, that what she dreaded most fell upon her: The reality of her aging body was exposed to an entire kingdom—to the subjects she obsessively longed to impress.

Granted, this queen lived in the world of fairy tales, but we respond to fictionalized stories because often they veil or decorate the truth in a manner palatable to us. They point to a malaise we may otherwise ignore; they compel us to listen to what we may otherwise resist. On this level, the naked queen represents a spiritual principle that befalls those who don't assess themselves from the truth of God's perspective. That principle is: whenever we believe a lie, eventually it wounds us. Especially when that lie is fabricated from other people's opinions and judgments. Particularly when the lie affects what we believe about ourselves.

Actually, a lie about ourselves rarely exists as a singular entity. Once an untruth has been uttered and embraced, it needs repetition and ancillary lies to keep it alive. Thomas Jefferson wrote to a friend, "He who permits himself to tell a lie once, finds it much easier to do it a second and third time, till at length it becomes habitual; he tells lies without attending to it, and truths without the world's believing him. This falsehood of the tongue leads to that of the heart, and in time depraves all of its good dispositions."[2] We stack up lie after lie, until we can no longer find, let alone recognize, the truth.

Like the queen who feared her subjects, we too readily believe in our physical shortcomings and unworthiness before a watching world. We believe our culture's lie that to be admired or even acceptable, we're to fit the media's hyped-up standard for beauty. Instead of trusting that we are created in God's image and redeemed through Christ; instead of appreciating what is good about our bodies; instead of living graciously and confidently in our own skin, we grovel in humanity's falsehoods.

Essentially, when we struggle with body image, when we gaze into the mirror and disparage what we see, when we say our physical selves are ugly or worthless, when we consider our looks less valuable than someone else's appearance, we are telling ourselves lies. We are refusing God's loving and redemptive view of us, of our bodies. We are wounding the soul and robbing ourselves of contentment, even enjoyment, regarding our unique presence in the world. We become habitual liars about our physical worth, plastering layer upon layer of falsehood on our self-esteem, immobilizing our movement into who God created us to be.

Though the lies are as varied and creative as the individual women who believe them, they always deny the goodness of God's creation and echo blame or self-pity or both. Often they sound like these statements:

"I'm ugly."

"I'm too flat-chested to be feminine."

"God must be mad at me because I'm fat."

"When I'm thin (or better looking), I'll be happy."

"I'm not attractive (or thin) enough for a man to love me."

"Because I'm not good looking, I'll never get what I want from life."

"My mother told me I'm homely, and she ruined me forever."

"God must not love me because He created me with . . . ."

"I'll never get over what kids said about me when I was a child."

"With as many flaws as I have, what's the use of taking care of myself?"

As outlined in earlier chapters, most of us learned these lies from our families and the culture, but through the years we probably added embellishments of our own. The reasons we cling to our "pet lies" may vary, but pinpointing our false beliefs—the beliefs that deny we were magnificently created by God and still reflect His image—can foster the process of casting them off. Indeed, uncovering and naming the lies we believe about our appearance is crucial to healing a wounded body image.

The Problem with Perception

Since I started a home business I've joked to my friends that I'm a woman of two extremes. Either I work at home in my comfortable bathrobe, or I don uncomfortable "dress-up clothes" for business appointments and speaking engagements. So it struck my funny bone when, sorting through old memorabilia, I found two forgotten photos of myself as a child. In one picture I'm wearing my favorite pair of pajamas: a one-piece, baggy clown suit made of flannel (which, incidentally, is still one of my preferable fabrics for nightwear). In the other photo I'm garbed in "make-believe, dress-up clothes." I'm wearing a long satin dress dotted with sequins, a fake mink stole and strappy high heels—all fashioned by my mom and the toy industry to fit my eight-year-old body.

At least now I know where these two opposite personas originated, I thought.

Later I showed the photos to a friend, expecting to laugh about them together.

"See? I've been a woman of extremes since childhood," I told her.

She looked at both photos and missing my point altogether, remarked, "You really were a cute kid."

"What? Me?" I asked, taking the photographs from her hands.

"Yes, you," she said. "Look at these; you're adorable."

"But I was fat!" I insisted.

"You don't look like it in these pictures," she countered. "You look normal."

"Well," I sputtered. "It's because I'm not standing next to my friends Becky and Kathy. I have pictures where I look fat next to them."

"Maybe they were skinny," she concluded.

This statement was so disparate from my beliefs about my childhood self, I couldn't think of another response. My mind went blank, probably due to the shock. Later I asked myself, *Had I been wrong about my looks all of these years? Even though I was overweight, was I not as huge as I thought I was? Had I overlooked the cute face, the impish grin? Had I missed out on what was pleasurable about my appearance?* Reluctantly and painfully, I had to say yes.

I also had to admit to ranking among "those women" I'd read about while researching females and body image. Some women consistently embrace negative messages about their appearance because the lies have penetrated so deep, they can no longer perceive the truth. They look in the mirror and can't see what is really there.

Body-image researchers have discovered that certain women *without* eating-disorder symptoms perceive themselves as one-fourth larger in size than they actually are. And the more inaccurate the perception, the worse they feel about themselves. Some overestimate their entire body, while others blow up specific body parts.[3] Additional research reveals that both men and women perceive themselves incorrectly, but females see themselves as bigger or "worse" looking than they actually are, while males see themselves as more fit and "better" looking than reality.[4] A rough translation: slender women perceive themselves as fat and fat men perceive themselves as slender. Men are more willing to believe they are good looking.

At least two rival theories exist to explain this distorted perception. Some researchers believe people who overestimate body size "have a visual-spatial problem in brain function that interferes with accurate perception." Other researchers say "the problem is emotional or cognitive: Size judgments are determined largely by what people feel or think about their bodies."[5] The latter is the more popular explanation. Either way, these people—particularly women—believe lies about themselves.

The Consistent Need to Cling

Other women cling to lies because to do otherwise would rattle their equilibrium. The authors of *Women and Self-Esteem*, who teach seminars on self-esteem around the country, explain that "human beings have an undeniable desire for consistency. When our internal thinking does not match our external experience, we have an uncanny way of manipulating the external until it aligns with our expectations. Women with low self-esteem are often extremely adept at this sort of manipulation.

"Beginning with a self-hypothesis such as 'I am unlovable,' a woman may set out to test and prove that hypothesis through experience. On general principle, of course, everyone would rather be proven right than wrong, so the woman who is sure she is unlovable will gather evidence that reaffirms her belief that yes, indeed, she is unlovable. She has created for herself a self-fulfilling prophecy. She gets what she most wanted—consistency—but only at the cost of her self-esteem and happiness."[6]

There are women—and I've been counted among them—who insist on believing the worst about their appearance, no matter what they see in the mirror or how much others reassure them of their acceptability. Have you ever complimented someone's appearance, only to have her object, "You must be kidding. I look like a wreck!"?

Have you ever participated in a dialogue like this?

"Oh, look at my face, it's awful!"

"No, it's not. You look good."

"But my nose—it's so big!"

"Your nose is fine. Really, quite normal."

"People stare at it . . ."

"No they don't; it's your imagination."

"Well, you just don't understand what it's like to have a big nose."

The truth is, the protesting woman doesn't want to believe that her nose or arms or thighs or stomach or whatever are acceptable or maybe even attractive. Letting go of this belief would mean that she is wrong; that she needs to change her appearance-related opinions, conversations and actions; that she will lose whatever perceived benefits she derives from putting down her appearance. Perhaps berating herself is the only way she knows to get attention or compliments, and she fears fading into the woodwork. Perhaps espousing her own brand of beauty would break a group or family code, making her different from the "norm" and an outcast. Perhaps believing in God's redemptive view of her would require too much change, too much work, too much of the unknown. Sticking with the familiar is easier. Perhaps acknowledging the truth—that she's wasted her time berating herself—might plunge her into grief. Or perhaps grief already is an old friend, and she doesn't want to give up emotionally suffering over her body.

"Strange though it seems, people become used to suffering, even though they may rebel against it," wrote Paul Tournier, the Swiss doctor who broke ground by integrating God's truth with psychological principles. "Some experience an odd feeling of depression just at the point where difficulties from which they have suffered cruelly are resolved. It is as if they could no longer do without suffering, or as if they found themselves weak, because their strength depended on reaction against suffering. After a long period of rain we find difficulty in believing that we shall ever see blue sky again, however much we may long for it. The same applies to the meteorology of the soul."[7]

Whatever the reason, be they apparent or deeply embedded within the psyche, when we hang on to negative attitudes about our bodies, we may gather attention but we rarely garner respect. People tire of propping up our self-esteem and doing the work for us that we're to accomplish for ourselves. If we're to find satisfaction with our appearance, we're the ones who need to instigate the change, do the work, feel the grief, take the risks, and tell the truth about ourselves. Passing the responsibility off to others, looking at ourselves through their viewfinders, depending on them to make the difference for us, only postpones the inner work that God asks of us. He wants each of us, deep within our souls, to know the truth so the truth can set us free (John 8:32).

A recently engaged friend told me, "You know, you should have a man in your life. Having a man love you makes you feel beautiful."

I nodded, but I only partially agree with her assumption. Yes, it is assuring to have people in our lives who believe we are lovely; it is wonderful when our "one special man" finds us desirable. I have experienced both feelings. But no one can substitute for the redemptive touch of God that enables us to believe it for ourselves.

Telling Ourselves the Truth

If lies about ourselves wound us, then conversely, the truth heals us. The truth can guide us away from the world's false assumptions into God's reality.

In his best-selling work, *The Road Less Traveled*, M. Scott Peck elaborates: "Truth is reality. That which is false is unreal. The more clearly we see the reality of the world, the better equipped we are to deal with the world. The less clearly we see the reality of the world—the more our minds are befuddled by falsehood, misperceptions and illusions—the less able we will be to determine correct courses of action and make wise decisions. Our view of reality is like a map with which to negotiate the terrain of life. If the map is true and accurate we will generally know where we are, and if we have decided where we want to go, we will generally know how to get there. If the map is false and inaccurate, we generally will be lost."[8]

When we decide to forsake the world's lies about ourselves, we can replace them with God's viewpoint. The Scriptures are His true and accurate roadmap for life, and from a biblical standpoint, we can soak in

God's good and purposeful intentions for our bodies. (Though I've referred to some of these Scriptures earlier, they bear repeating so they'll sink into our souls.) For example, we can confidently say to ourselves:

- *I am created by God, and what He created was very good.* "God saw all that he had made, and it was very good" (Gen. 1:31).

- *I am created in God's image.* "So God created man in his own image, in the image of God he created him; male and female he created them" (Gen. 1:27).

- *I am a wonderful creation.* "For you created my inmost being; you knit me together in my mother's womb. I praise you because I am fearfully and wonderfully made; your works are wonderful, I know that full well" (Ps. 139:13-14).

- *I am who God planned me to be.* "My frame was not hidden from you when I was made in the secret place. When I was woven together in the depths of the earth, your eyes saw my unformed body. All the days ordained for me were written in your book before one of them came to be" (Ps. 139:15-16).

If we have accepted God's plan of redemption through Christ, then we can also claim these statements as our own:

- *I am a temple for God's Spirit.* "Don't you know that you yourselves are God's temple and that God's Spirit lives in you? If anyone destroys God's temple, God will destroy him; for God's temple is sacred, and you are that temple" (1 Cor. 3:16-17).

- *I am joined with Christ's body.* "Do you not know
  that your bodies are members of Christ himself?"
  (1 Cor. 6:15).

These are glorious physical and spiritual truths that
lift our heads and hearts upward. At the same time, we
live with the reality that our earthly bodies are short-
lived and diminished by age, disease, accidents, and
other effects of sin's roam of the world. So with per-
plexity we may ask, "If I am fearfully and wonderfully
made, why do I have an obvious physical deformity?"
Or, "If I am created in God's image, why is my body
aging?" Shouldn't it be one way or the other?

No. Not as long as we live on the earth. Because of
the Fall, we carry both the mark of God and the effects
of sin in our bodies. Likewise, living with a broken
earth's realities and accepting God's redemptive view
of us are not mutually exclusive activities. Rather, if we
are to loose ourselves from body-image bondage, one
action depends upon the other. When the mirror
reflects the Fall's effects on our bodies, we must remember that God views us with loving eyes. Based on His
acceptance, we can move our minds from an earth-
trapped to a spiritually-freeing perspective. We can further affirm scriptural truth by saying:

- *I know God values the heart more than appearance.*
  "The Lord does not look at the things man looks
  at. Man looks at the outward appearance, but the
  Lord looks at the heart" (1 Sam. 16:7).
- *I have a treasure within an earthen vessel.* "For God,
  who said, 'Let light shine out of darkness,' made
  his light shine in our hearts to give us the light of
  the knowledge of the glory of God in the face of
  Christ. But we have this treasure in jars of clay to

show that this all-surpassing power is from God and not from us" (2 Cor. 4:6-7).

- *I can renew my inner person, though the outer person decays.* "Therefore we do not lose heart. Though outwardly we are wasting away, yet inwardly we are being renewed day by day" (2 Cor. 4:16).

- *I know God has compassion for my bodily predicaments.* "As a father has compassion on his children, so the Lord has compassion on those who fear him; for he knows how we are formed, he remembers that we are dust" (Ps. 103:13-14).

- *I am to look at eternal things that are unseen.* "So we fix our eyes not on what is seen, but on what is unseen. For what is seen is temporary, but what is unseen is eternal. Now we know that if the earthly tent we live in is destroyed, we have a building from God, an eternal house in heaven, not built by human hands" (2 Cor. 4:18—5:1).

- *I will be transformed and perfected in heaven.* "But our citizenship is in heaven. And we eagerly await a Savior from there, the Lord Jesus Christ, who, by the power that enables him to bring everything under his control, will transform our lowly bodies so that they will be like his glorious body" (Phil. 3:20-21).

As we remind ourselves of scriptural truths, we can ask the Holy Spirit to cleanse our souls, flushing out the world's opinions, replacing them with spiritual reality. We can also remember that supplanting lies with the truth isn't a once-for-all act. To keep the truth flowing in our minds and hearts, we need to wash in God's Word frequently. Most of all, we need the supernatural influence of the Holy Spirit so we can truly hear, understand,

and change from the inside out. And if we ask for this in His name, He will do it (John 14:13).

Working Through the Madness

Jan is a counselor who guides a support group affectionately called the Mad Women's Club. "I laughingly say these are women in their forties who wake up mad one morning and don't get over it," she says. "Since I'm a few years beyond that age, I can laugh with them and say, 'I know it's tough being in the hormonally-challenged generation.' Reality is, the problem is usually not a lack of hormones but a deception they have believed and refused to let go."

To work through these women's "madness," Jan explains, "usually it takes consistent repetition of the truth to make headway in these situations because the women's attitudes have been frozen for a long time." In their sessions Jan keeps repeating the truths that counter the lies these women hold on to. "These women remind me of the person who grabs a hot electrical wire and, although it is killing him, he can't let it go. The same source that made touching a hot wire dangerous is the problem that holds him fastened to the wire."[9]

I respect Jan's wise and pragmatic approach to guiding these women toward the truth. She doesn't tell them to stuff their feelings; she gives them permission to be angry, to grieve the losses of believing in lies. She understands that grieving opens the gate for healing to enter in.

When we awaken to the world's lies about body image we need a time to grieve our losses—to bellow loudly or to sit remorsefully alone, or anything in between that acknowledges our wounds. What we grieve may vary from woman to woman. We can grieve the lies we've told ourselves and the negative body messages others have heaped upon us. We can be angry that the world told us beauty is paramount. We can feel sorrow for our physical limitations and the body parts we've so often berated. We can mourn the time lost to obsessing about our appearance.

I remember the pain I felt while looking at photographs of myself in my twenties and thirties, realizing I was more attractive than I gave myself credit for during that time. I spent those years putting down my looks when I could have enjoyed a face and body not yet introduced to the signs of aging. I didn't correctly perceive what the mirror reflected back to me, nor did I let myself bask in God's love and acceptance. I believed the world's lies that no matter how good we look, it is never enough.

After recognizing this loss I grieved silently, for that fits my personality, but I've a friend who has grieved with a Waldenesque twist she calls "loud desperation." There really is no correct way to dump out the past, but our grief is to be confined to a season. If we nurture grief and anger too long, it turns to bitterness and the pain paralyzes us.

Forgiveness is also essential to this process: forgiving ourselves; forgiving the family and others who contributed to our negative self-image; forgiving a culture that pressures us toward body obsession. We might spend time forgiving ourselves for judging other people's appearance, or asking God to forgive us for maligning His handiwork and sinning against Him, to wipe away the body shame within us, and to heal us. With the prophet Isaiah we can claim, "[Jesus] was pierced for our transgressions, he was crushed for our iniquities; the punishment that brought us peace was upon him, *and by his wounds we are healed*" (Isa. 53:5, italics mine). We can be assured that "anyone who trusts in him *will never be put to shame*" (Rom. 10:11, italics mine).

Some of us will pass through this process alone or with a therapist; others will want the input of a support or Bible study group. Some may need the deep work of breaking a spiritual bondage. Whatever we need, however we pursue it, this inner work can lead us to a turning point—a time when we're willing to forsake self-flagellation and live above the destructive opinions and judgments of others. In biblical terms, this is repentance, the act of changing our minds and walking in a different direction. It promises a new life ahead.

Protecting Our Progress

A few months ago I ate breakfast with a friend who, after reading a book about our culture's beauty myth, decided to think differently about her body. "I decided I don't need to be slim to be happy," she explained. "I feel much better when I allow my body to be fuller and more womanly." But when we met again a month later, her attitude had changed, at least on that day. She felt unhappy with her weight and talked about dieting.

My friend learned that letting go of our culture's beauty imperative is a three-steps-forward and two-steps-backward process. Old habits die slowly, and cultural influences pervade everywhere. We will be constantly challenged and won't always respond to the "be thin, be beautiful" pressure the way we know or want to. So we need to measure ourselves by progress rather than perfection.

This is never so clear to me as when I prepare to speak in front of a group. Suddenly my contentment crashes, and my hair, makeup, weight, even how I pluck my eyebrows seems all wrong. I remember that people no longer compliment my eyes or say I look younger than my age. I fear that if I don't measure up to the audience's appearance standards my message will be ignored. At a recent conference when my hair wouldn't "pouf" but my eyelids did, I stood in front of the mirror, reminding myself of God's pleasure in me, regardless of what I looked like. Before I spoke to this group of five hundred women, I had to let my "head knowledge" once again soak into my heart.

The Bible reminds us "to be made new in the attitude of your minds; and to put on the new self, created to be like God in true righteousness and holiness" (Eph. 4:23-24). This constitutes a daily renewal, remembering that whenever we stand against the world's thinking, we are engaged in a spiritual battle. "For our struggle is not against flesh and blood, but against the rulers, against the authorities, against the powers of this dark world and against the spiritual forces of evil in the heavenly realms" (Eph. 6:12). Never forget that Satan wants us so trapped in appearance anxieties that we neglect our relationship with God and sharing His love with others.

For this reason, we're to protect our progress, choosing behaviors that reflect our repentance and guarding against influences that drag us back into faulty thinking about our bodies. Again, for each of us the actions will differ, but the following are examples of how we can nourish our redeemed outlook on body image. I've had to practice many of these ideas myself.

- Accept compliments graciously, without disagreeing or pointing out what's "wrong" with our appearance.
- Stop making self-deprecating remarks, even if they are said jokingly.
- Appreciate and compliment other women's appearance without comparing them to ourselves.
- Watch fewer television shows that parade the beauty imperative in front of us.
- Monitor the magazines we read, refusing to steep ourselves in the world's mindset about bodies and beauty.
- Transition women's conversation about appearance to other topics, particularly when the comments are negative.
- Devote less time to browsing clothing and department stores, dwelling on the need to fit an advertised "look."
- Spend less time with people who obsess about body image and judge others according to their appearance.
- Quit begging for reassurance about our appearance.
- Believe the people who tell us we look beautiful to them.
- Regularly review what the Scriptures say about our value.
- Place the emphasis on health instead of beauty.

With these suggestions, I'm not implying that we forsake all attention to our appearance: never wearing makeup, not shopping for enhancing clothes, neglecting to groom and care for our bodies. Instead, with God's help we can abandon negativism and obsessiveness about our appearance, substituting it with a reasonable approach. For some of us this means finally being able to look into the mirror; for others, it means looking in the mirror a lot less. For all of us, it means responding from an inner centeredness based on eternal truths, rather than caving in to fleeting and erroneous opinions. We can accept and appreciate ourselves—not for who we once were, or who we hope to become, but for who we are now.

Then, when we've invested in this internal transformation, we can better respond to faulty opinions and pressures from others.

Responding to Faulty Opinions

"Imagine this: You get up in the morning, turn on the TV and as you dress for work, you listen to the news being reported by an anchorwomen who wears a size twenty. On the bus to work, you flip through your favorite magazine, which this month, miraculously, contains no ads that use women's bodies to sell products. During your coffee break, you enjoy the company of the other women in your office, and not one of you, even for a moment, talks about dieting or weight . . .

"Does all this sound improbable, even impossible? Improbable, perhaps. Impossible? *No.* This scenario is a potential that may have to wait for our daughter's daughter's daughter's time, but it *is* a possibility and it *can* happen—if we lay the groundwork. Until that time arrives, all of us have to figure out how to handle what comes flying at us in all directions from a misogynistic culture that tells women to shrink their bodies and curb their appetites."[10]

This dream for the future belongs to two female psychotherapists who counsel women with eating disorders, but their advice applies to all of us. When we adopt an accepting attitude toward our bodies, there are people for whom our appearance won't be an issue either. But what about the people who won't accept how we look? The ones who criticize and suggest how to change ourselves? The ones who reject us?

Responding to them isn't easy, especially when they're intimately involved in our lives, but I have a few "starter" suggestions. First, we can review both God's and our own acceptance of ourselves, then from a place of internal assurance we can ask these questions:

Does it matter what they think?

A guy on the street wisecracks about the size of our breasts. A clerk at the cosmetics counter points out our facial flaws. Women in an infomercial talk about how horrible it is to have wrinkles or cellulite or untoned thighs. In the long run (or even in the short run), do we need to care about what they think? Not really. We're wasting energy when we let people "out there" affect how we feel about ourselves. They don't know the real, wise and lovable us. They're not in charge of our lives. And obviously, they're ignorant about what really matters in life.

On the other hand, if someone who matters to us communicates disapproval, then we can ask the next question.

Whose problem is this?

When people pick at or joke about our appearance, the problem is theirs, not ours. There is no excuse for maligning and disrespecting another person—a unique being created by God—and quite frankly, body bashers and judgers haven't matured emotionally. These are hard words if the people are mothers, fathers, husbands, siblings, or children; our lives enmesh with theirs constantly, and we care about them. Yet to live apart from "bad body thoughts" about ourselves, we need to mentally pull back and assign "the problem" to the guilty persons. No matter how much we love them or want their respect, these people have their own unresolved issues.

"When others make comments about your body, they are actually having bad body thoughts of their own. They are disguising some private, personal, painful feeling," explain psychotherapists Jane Hirschmann and Carol Munter. "No matter how hard you have been trying to question [their] assumptions, or how diligently you have tried to break the body-bashing habit, these [opinions] can trigger an old response that makes it extremely difficult to hold your ground and to recognize that what you are dealing with is simply another bad body thought situation.

"What you must come to understand is that, this time, it is [someone else] who is having the bad body thought. He or she is using your body to communicate his or her own issue. This issue may have nothing whatsoever to do with you or it may involve you in some tangential way, but rest assured, it is not about the shape of your body."[11]

Usually the issue is connected to these people's low self-esteem and perceived lack of control, and while we can't be responsible for their negativity—they need to "own" their pain and work toward healing—we can choose not to let it penetrate us.

How can I speak up?

Too often when people criticize our appearance, we fall silent because they're affirming our fears about ourselves. But if we allow ourselves the freedom of body acceptance, we gain a strength that can "talk back" to these people's jokes and criticisms. Not in a revengeful way that spouts, "So what's it to yah?", but in a calm and gracious manner, we can educate them about our self-acceptance and their disrespect.

We can respond like this: "I feel good about the way I look, so why is it a problem for you?" Or, "Why is appearance such an issue for you?" Or, "When you make those comments, you are disrespecting me. Why is that?" Or, "When you say these things, do you mean to hurt me? Why do you want to do that?" These and similar responses can help people recognize their rudeness and possibly open a dialogue about the real issues at hand.

How can I pray for their healing?

Ask God to work in these people's souls, healing insecurities and changing critical attitudes. Be steadfast in your own beliefs without attacking them, quietly praying that they will repent of their sin.

"Our culture hasn't only affected women, it has affected men deeply, too, and everyone's suffering as a result," explains Debra Evans, author of *Beauty and the Best*. "What's needed today is the far-reaching realization that many of today's beliefs and attitudes about beauty fit our culture, not Scripture. Men and women alike need to repent for serving the false gods associated with physical attractiveness and personal appearance. In humility, we need to ask God's forgiveness, and move toward a higher calling."[12]

Knowing Who We Are

In the film, *Circle of Friends,* a plump high school girl develops a relationship with a popular and handsome male classmate. He is impressed that despite her physique, she expresses a confidence about herself.

At one point he asks, "You really know who you are, don't you?"

"Of course," she replies incredulously. "Why wouldn't I?"[13]

For me, this interaction sums up a redemptive relationship to our bodies. If we know the Creator of the universe, if He accepts us lovingly and wholeheartedly, then why shouldn't we? Why wouldn't we be confident in who He created us to be?

"We can be confident in our uniqueness," writes author Ingrid Trobisch. "To become the one I am created to be, isn't that my great work in life?"[14]

The answer is yes, both for our souls and for our bodies.

Chapter Six

THE ART OF CHANGE

Discerning between pride and stewardship.

After my bath each day I examined my naked body in the mirror, and every day I noticed new wrinkles. So I underwent massages, dieted, and performed strenuous gymnastics to hold off age. But I was not successful.

—Greta Garbo, Actress

By the fall, I was into my jeans. And proud of it. I was ready to tell the world how I'd done it. I wanted to share my secret with everyone else who'd struggled. So I went on the air and blew out the Optifast lines that day. Heaven only knows how much money we made for them.

When people would criticize me and say, "Don't worry, she'll put the weight back on," I couldn't imagine what they were talking about. I thought it impossible. Anybody who had shown as much discipline as I had by not eating for four months certainly had licked this problem for good. What I *didn't know was that my metabolism was shot. I'd lost muscle weight. There was nothing my body could have done but gain weight.*

I weighed 142 pounds when I put on the jeans. It was time to stop taking the supplement and return to real food. I was 142 for one day. The next day I was 145. In two weeks, I was 155. I remember being invited to a party at Don Johnson's house in Aspen and not going because I thought, at 155, I was much too fat for a party with Hollywood types. Oh no, it was starting again. I felt helpless.

—Oprah Winfrey, *Talk Show Host*

Recently I commemorated the Academy Awards presentation with a group of women who spanned five generations. While eating lasagna, bread, salad, and brownies, we sat in front of a big screen television to watch the pre-show arrivals of the rich, famous, and usually talented celebrities of our era.

Along with the on-camera interviewer, we sized up the "beautiful people" before the official show began. The interviewer's favorite question to a celebrity was, "Who are you wearing?" and each actor dutifully responded with the name of his or her outfit's designer. After this, it was hard to hear the rest of the interviewer-celebrity exchange because our group's commentary, ranging from the ridiculous to the sublime, rose in volume. We paid particular attention to the attractive women, presiding as both jury and judge over their Oscar night appearance.

"Isn't she just exquisite?"

"Look at that dress . . . only she could pull off that look."

"Yuck. Where did she get that gown? A mistake!"

"Don't you think her arms look flabby?"

"Guys think she's so great looking, but I just don't get it."

"Do you think she had a face lift?" (The reply: "I certainly hope so, or I'm going to be depressed.")

"I can't believe someone like her doesn't have a date tonight."

We were a true irony: dressed in grubbies and stuffing our faces with food while scrutinizing and sporadically criticizing some of the most beautiful women in the world. "This is a tough crowd to play," quipped one of the women reclining on the floor, referring to our group. We laughed. She certainly was right, and her comment made me pause.

Why am I participating in this commentary? I asked myself. *I know better than this.* Part of me wanted to admire the gorgeous women on the screen; another part felt tinges of envy; still another part dislikes the star system that insists beauty is important. The combination prompted me to place high expectations on these women, as if to say, "All right, if you're going to play this beauty game, than I'm going to expect you to be perfect!"

How did I get caught up in this? I wondered. I'd come to socialize with friends and instead focused on appearances.

Later, while driving home alone, I felt ashamed. I asked God to forgive me for my critical spirit and for slipping into the world's attitudes about bodies and appearance. I reminded myself of the diligence needed to keep viewing me and others through God's eyes, especially when I'm exposed to the spectacle of beauty.

And I questioned whether it had been wise for me to plop in front of that giant television at all.

As I've thought about that night I've been struck by the powerful allure of the beauty quest and how it raises conflicting feelings within us. We appreciate beauty for its sheer loveliness; we resent beauty for its demands on us. We look at the world's glamorous women and expect them to change whatever isn't "right" about them; we understand how difficult it can be to change ourselves. We have a list of things we'd like to alter about our appearance; we'd like not to *have to* change anything. We get confused about how much change is too much or how much change is too little. So what are we to do?

Even when we have adopted the Creator's redemptive view of us, we still can't escape the question, "How much time and energy do I put into my appearance?" As with other aspects of our relationship with God, He deals with us individually. As much as we'd like an easy, cookie-cutter answer, He wants to respond personally, to envelop this decision within an already intimate relationship with Him. My opinion is that His guidance to each of us is unique, depending on our circumstances, our need for inner healing, and our attitudes of the heart. However, there are two conditions we all need to confront honestly before answering the "to change or not to change?" question. These are the ugliness of pride and the responsibility of stewardship.

The Sufficiency of God

Recently a member of my prayer team, who often speaks at women's retreats, faxed this note to me, querying about my recent speaking engagement.

Dear Judy,

How did your conference go? I prayed for you all weekend while I was doing mine in St. Louis. I had quite an experience getting there. At the airport, going up the stone steps to my gate, I tripped and heard the awful sound made as my two front teeth chipped off against the next step up.

Of course, I split my lip. Oh, I was a real doll all weekend! Strangely enough, I think it was the most blessed weekend of ministry in my life. The women had absolutely bathed, covered that weekend in prayer, and that is what made all the difference. I could see God had me prepare perfectly for their needs. It was an obvious meshing, like with gears.

Now the dentist has remade my teeth and my lip is healing, and what I will remember is that God hates pride. He certainly dealt with mine in a dramatic way. I tell you, I did go on chastened, clutching my ice cube in a couple of Kleenexes to my bloody lip.

Blessings on you, Win.

I cringed inwardly when I read about Win's accident, asking myself, *Would I have continued through the weekend as graciously as she did?* Probably not. I would have wanted to "milk it for all it's worth," and catch the next plane home with lips tightly pursed together. Win's example chastened my own pride about appearance. I realized that even though I'm not questing for perfection, I expect the "minimum requirements" to be in order when I'm facing the public; i.e. my teeth are brushed and certainly not chipped; my lipstick looks smooth and my lips are not bleeding . . . especially when that public is sitting in rows of seats, looking directly at me!

Yet God asked Win to press on when her appearance suddenly slipped to what the world considers "below par." He employed her as a vessel of spiritual beauty to meet the needs of other women. Now let me be clear: I don't think God said, "Today I'm going to chip Win's teeth and humiliate her." I don't think He *caused* the accident (we humans are adept at tripping on our own), but I know He *used* an unfortunate situation to remind His child of His sufficiency. Christ said, "My grace is sufficient for you, for my power is made perfect in weakness" (2 Cor. 12:9). God doesn't use us based on what we look like: He uses us based on the condition of our souls. Above all, He looks for humble hearts.

The Ugliness of Pride

Though I don't consider Win a prideful woman, she knew what resided within her. So it is for us. But even if people draw attention to our pride, they probably point to the tip of the iceberg—to what peeks out at the world. Only God's illumination reveals how deeply and widely pride penetrates our souls. In regard to appearance, we can take pride for granted, being expected to revel in our good looks. From well-meaning people we're told to have pride in our physical presentation. We're reminded to make a good first impression; if we've got it, we're to flaunt it. But Win is right: God hates pride.

"I hate pride and arrogance," says the Lord in Proverbs 8:13, ranking it along with "evil behavior and perverse speech." Earlier in Proverbs King Solomon, who was well-acquainted with personal pride, warned, "There are six things the Lord hates, seven that are detestable to him: haughty eyes, a lying tongue, hands that shed innocent blood, a heart that devises wicked schemes, feet that are quick to rush into evil, a false witness who pours out lies and a man who stirs up dissension among brothers" (Prov. 6:16-19). It's sobering to note that pride's "haughty eyes" is listed first and considered as detestable as lying, murder, and wicked schemes. Even as I type out these verses, my mind doesn't fully grasp God's abhorrence for this sin. Pride is so much a part of our culture's persona. It has been so integrated into my own lifestyle.

Still, God hates pride, no matter how beautifully it's packaged. He hates pride so much, He allows it to lead to our downfall (Prov. 16:18). Isaiah warned the women of Judah who worshipped beauty that the Lord would harshly judge them. When I review what the prophet said to these women, I can't ignore that we have similar female attitudes within our culture.

> The Lord says, "The women of Zion are haughty, walking along with outstretched necks, flirting with their eyes, tripping along with mincing steps, with ornaments jingling on their ankles.
> "Therefore the Lord will bring sores on the heads of the women of Zion; the Lord will make their scalps bald."
> In that day the Lord will snatch away their finery: the bangles and headbands and crescent necklaces, the earrings and bracelets and veils, the headdresses and ankle chains and sashes, the perfume bottles and charms, the signet rings and nose rings, the fine robes and the capes and cloaks, the purses and

mirrors, and the linen garments and tiaras and shawls.

Instead of fragrance there will be a stench; instead of a sash, a rope; instead of well-dressed hair, baldness; instead of fine clothing, sackcloth; instead of beauty, branding.

Your men will fall by the sword, your warriors in battle.

The gates of Zion will lament and mourn; destitute, she will sit on the ground.

In that day seven women will take hold of one man and say, 'We will eat our own food and provide our own clothes; only let us be called by your name. Take away our disgrace!'" (Isa. 3:16–4:1).

God wasn't angry with these women because they owned fine apparel and jewelry. In the Old Testament, when people obeyed the Lord, often He blessed them materially.[1] The Lord's wrath burned against these women because they made beauty their god, usurping His rightful place in their lives. A Bible commentator explains their offense: "The women of Judah had placed their emphasis on clothing and jewelry rather than on God. They dressed to be noticed, to gain approval, and to be fashionable. Yet they ignored the real purpose of their lives. Instead of being concerned about the oppression around them (3:14-15), they were self-serving and self-centered."[2]

After the Lord stated His complaint against these women, the prophet described a different outcome for those who follow and obey their Creator. The subsequent verses indicate that pride, beauty, and glory belong to God, but He will forgive proud people if they repent. He longs to make them holy.

> In that day the Branch of the Lord will be beautiful and glorious, and the fruit of the land will be the pride and glory of the survivors in Israel.
> Those who are left in Zion, who remain in Jerusalem, will be called holy, all who are recorded among the living in Jerusalem.
> The Lord will wash away the filth of the women of Zion; he will cleanse the bloodstains from Jerusalem by a spirit of judgment and a spirit of fire (Isa. 4:2-4).

We may not be "tripping along with mincing feet" or wearing nose rings and tiaras, but we can remember God loathes pride. So when we're devoting time to grooming ourselves and changing our appearance, we can ask, "Is my pride wrapped up in this?" (Does it bother us when people don't notice how nice we look? Are we upset if we don't think we look presentable to others? Are we overly style conscious and designer-label dependent? Are we constantly dieting?) We can also recognize that pride isn't always overt; dwelling on what we consider our "unbeautiful" features or defiantly "dressing down" can be pride in disguise. The reverse snobbery of anti-fashion is still snobbery.

With such harsh words from God about pride, at this juncture we could throw up our hands and say, "What's the use? It sounds as though caring at all about my appearance is sin! Am I never to wear makeup? Color my hair? Get a manicure? Do I have to look like a slob to follow God?" Certainly not. There is a difference between appreciating our bodies and obsessing about them, and to care for our physical selves is an act of biblical stewardship.

The Body Resplendent

Either way we observe it—as a whole entity or breaking it down into parts—the human body is a resplendent masterpiece. Think just of the skeleton, an artistic yet functional armature for God's creative work. The average woman's skeleton contains 206 bones. Twenty-nine fused bones construct the skull, which protects the brain and sensory organs. Twenty-four vertebrae form a spinal column, which supports the body's trunk and head. Rigid bones meet at the joints and are classified as ball-and-socket joints (hips and shoulders), gliding joints (hands), hinge joints (elbows, knees), or saddle joints (thumb), according to the type of movement they provide. The "stuff" of which bones are formed is a complicated layering of Creator-made materials. The outer layer of the bone is a hard periosteum. Beneath are cells called osteocytes, embedded within a thin, mineralized, platelike structure called lamella. The bone's inner surface is the endosteum, which surrounds the marrow cavity in which cells and platelets form.

Ligaments, made of a fibrous tissue, bind together the bone ends and cordlike tendons "convey the power of locomotion from muscle to bone."[3] A woman's body contains more than 600 muscles, accounting for about 40 percent of her body weight. These muscles are classified as either skeletal (they have voluntary movement or are under conscious control), smooth (partly involuntary movement), or cardiac (involuntary movement). Another 20 to 25 percent of a women's weight consists of fat, which is essential for fertility. In fact, to be fertile a woman must carry at least 16 percent body fat to create the necessary hormone production.

Traveling to the outside of the body, the surface area of a woman's skin is between 15 and 20 square feet. On the average, every one-square inch of female skin contains 15 feet of blood vessels, 12 feet of nerves, 1,500 sensory receptors, 650 sweat glands, 100 oil glands and over three million cells. The life cycle of skin is about 28 days, so we're constantly shedding and renewing our outer layer. (It's been claimed that 90 percent of household dust is actually dead skin.)

For females, on the head alone there are approximately one hundred thousand hairs. Each hair is a flexible filament, growing out of a pocketlike hair follicle embedded in the skin. "The outer surface of each hair consists of layers of flattened, overlapping scales that form the cuticle. Beneath the cuticle is a middle layer, the cortex, which is made of several layers of flattened cells."[4] The medulla, or the central core, comprises large cells separated by air spaces. Hair color depends on the range of melanin pigments produced by more specialized cells, called melanocytes, at a hair follicle's base. The pigment granules transfer to the cells of the hair shaft. Varying sizes and densities of melanin granules determine whether the hair projects shades of black, blonde, brown or red.[5]

I won't continue with this recital on the amazingly detailed human body. It'd take too long to finish, and like me, most women have seen physiology charts posted in medical offices and have marveled, at least briefly, at our physical complexities. Yet to truly appreciate God's gift to each of us, it helps to periodically remind ourselves of the intricate and remarkable "house" we live in and carry around every moment, every day. The philosopher Sophocles wrote, "Numberless are the world's wonders, but none—none more wondrous than the body of man."[6] And later the poet and playwright William Shakespeare exclaimed, "What a piece of work is a man! How noble in reason! How infinite in faculties! In form and moving how express and admirable! in action how like an angel, in apprehension how like a god!"[7]

For the most part, though, we take for granted our functions and movements, expecting our bodies to perform what we want, when we want it done. At least until a bodily part deteriorates or malfunctions. Then as we seek healing we're overwhelmed by the detail, terminology, and mystery woven into our component parts. In addition, the pain or merely the annoyance of a malfunction can serve as a wake-up call to become more appreciative and better stewards of our bodies. In my case, with the onset of chronic back problems, I've become intrigued by how the bones and muscles operate, and I'm grateful for even a half day without pain. I'm also interested in recapturing my overall flexibility—a problem I never thought about in years past. Through experience I now know if I don't use it, I'll lose it.

The Responsibility of Stewardship

To keep our marvelous bodies in good working order, health practitioners recommend we practice preventative and maintenance habits such as eating healthy foods, getting enough sleep, finding time to exercise, having medical checkups, taking vitamins and minerals. And of course, they recommend corrective measures: allowing ourselves to heal from injuries, paying attention to troubling symptoms, pursuing the means to recover from disease and illness. For all humans there are cause-and-effect reasons to care for ourselves and make appropriate changes if our physical well-being is threatened. If we don't pay attention to our bodies, they will eventually rebel against us, apart from the natural deterioration due to aging.

However, there are additional and higher reasons for practicing good stewardship toward our bodies. "We are made in the image of God. For us, the shell of skin and muscle and bones serve as a vessel, a repository of His image," reminds Dr. Paul Brand, a medical doctor. "We can comprehend and even convey something of the Creator. Our cellular constructions of proteins arranged by DNA can become temples of the Holy Spirit. We are not 'mere mortals.' We are, all of us, immortals."[8]

While we're all created in God's image, only those who've repented of their sins and have received Christ as Savior become the temples of God's Spirit. This is a sacred keeping that affects our whole being—body, soul, spirit—but again, we can overlook how the Spirit's indwelling should affect the way we treat our bodies. Several times in the New Testament Paul reminded Christians of this relationship.

> Therefore, I urge you, brothers, in view of
> God's mercy, to offer your bodies as living

sacrifices, holy and pleasing to God—this is your spiritual act of worship (Rom. 12:1).

Do you not know that your bodies are members of Christ himself? (1 Cor. 6:15).

Do you not know that your body is a temple of the Holy Spirit, who is in you, whom you have received from God? You are not your own; you were bought at a price. Therefore honor God with your body (1 Cor. 6:19-20).

Do you not know that in a race all the runners run, but only one gets the prize? Run in such a way as to get the prize.

Everyone who competes in the games goes into strict training. They do it to get a crown that will not last; but we do it to get a crown that will last forever.

Therefore I do not run like a man running aimlessly; I do not fight like a man beating the air.

No, I beat my body and make it my slave so that after I have preached to others, I myself will not be disqualified for the prize (1 Cor. 9:24-27).

If we examine the context of these verses, we learn that several of them refer to keeping our bodies free from sin, but these Scriptures also hold ramifications for staying in good physical condition. Though Christian martyrs have died in both his times and ours, for most of us Paul speaks metaphorically about "sacrificing" and "beating" our bodies. Collectively, he admonished believers to live with a discipline that doesn't allow bodily appetites to control us. Rather, we are to control the body. But take note: Paul does not describe the body obsessiveness prevalent in our culture, nor the addictive characteristic of a disorder. This is a discipline that frees the Holy Spirit to work within and through us. We are free to run the spiritual race, fulfilling God's purposes without being hindered by a preoccupation with our bodies and appearance.

After telling Roman Christians to offer their bodies as living sacrifices to God, Paul then wrote: "Do not conform any longer to the pattern of this world, but be transformed by the renewing of your mind. Then you will be able to test and approve what God's will is—his good, pleasing and perfect will. For by the grace given me I say to every one of you: Do not think of yourself more highly than you ought, but rather think of yourself with sober judgment, in accordance with the measure of faith God has given you" (Rom. 12:2-3). Applying these verses to our physicality, we can humbly place our personal body care in proper perspective to accomplishing God's will and work in the world.

Once again, for some of us this balance means we spend much less time analyzing and working on our bodies, giving up an addiction to workouts or excessive grooming habits. For others, it means spending more time taking care of ourselves. For example, I hate to exercise. If somebody called me a couch potato I'd reply, "Please bring the butter and sour cream." While writing this book, however, I've been convicted about my sedentary ways. Though I've grown comfortable and accepting of who God made me to be; though I'm not feeling compelled to be thin or even lose weight, I need to undergird my health. If I'm to fulfill God's purpose for me, and that mission includes speaking to groups, my body needs to be stronger and more flexible, able to manage the rigors of travel and the pressure of meeting unfamiliar people's needs. For my denial in this area of health, for my lack of preparation for God's plan, I've needed to repent.

Finding a Humble Balance

So where does all of this explanation leave us? Hopefully, with the understanding that caring for our bodies, even changing our appearance, is a matter of balance. While we accept our bodies for who God made them to be, we still have a responsibility to take care of them reasonably. Not with pride, but with an attitude of humility and gratitude. We can enjoy our glorious bodies without becoming slaves to them. We can appreciate the bodies given to other people, without feeling envious or critical. We can believe our bodies are not an end in themselves, but a means for letting the Holy Spirit dwell within and pursuing God's purpose for us. We can allow the caring and feeding of our bodies to set us free from worrying about our appearance.

This is my ultimate goal: to be set free. Before God I want my grooming, clothing, eating, and exercising habits to be a settled matter that allows me to get over body self-consciousness and to get on with my life, operating at a healthy capacity, becoming all I'm meant to be. I want to remember Paul's advice: "Therefore, since we are surrounded by such a great cloud of witnesses, let us throw off everything that hinders and the sin that so easily entangles, and let us run with perseverance the race marked out for us. Let us fix our eyes on Jesus, the author and perfecter of our faith" (Heb. 12:1-2). But God doesn't reserve this release from hindrances just for me; He desires that we all be set free.

So when we consider tending to our appearance and making changes, we can ask, "Is this pride or stewardship?" and allow the Holy Spirit to provide the answer. His reply may change as we progress through the varying stages of our lives. For instance, in my early thirties I was a clothes addict. I spent large amounts of money on clothing, wanting to own quality everything. I was determined to be the best-dressed woman at work and spent considerable time mixing and matching so I'd gather attention and compliments. My identity hung on satin-padded hangers and it took several years before I let God release me from their clutches. Definitely, buying clothes was an issue of pride for me.

To the virtual disbelief of my long-term friends, these days clothing hasn't mattered much to me. Because I work at home I'm edging perilously close to becoming a permanent slouch, and as an act of stewardship I need to confess my laziness and "spiff up my act." To me it's humorous that God's message to me about clothing is considerably different than it was a decade ago.

The "pride or stewardship?" principle can be applied to many of the questions we ask about tending to and changing our appearance. "Should I lose weight?" "How many makeup and skin care products do I really need?" "Is it all right to get plastic surgery?" "How much time and money will I spend at the gym?" "What clothes should I buy? How much money should I spend on them?" "Why did I buy so much jewelry?" "Do I really need four new dresses?" "By doing this, who am I trying to please?"

The possible questions from women seem unlimited, but when we consider our own personal queries, it's vital that we answer from an internal centeredness on God and His loving acceptance, not from a desire to fill up what's spiritually missing inside of us. We can remind ourselves that pride leads to self-criticism, obsession, and addiction. Stewardship allows us to accept and appreciate ourselves, even when we need to make changes. It sets us free to do and to be.

At the height of my clothes addiction, my mother said to me, "Judy, you're just trying to fill up the hole that's inside of you." It was the truth, and she wanted it to set me free. Now I can own nice clothes without the clothes owning me.

However, with this question-asking I don't want to minimize the complexity of recovering from eating disorders, physical abuse, or other deeply scarring body issues. In these instances it is always God's desire that we be released from them. The "pride or stewardship?" question becomes moot; if we'd ask it, the words would sound painfully frivolous. For women plodding through these issues, the art of change focuses on deep inner healing, not on whether they'll make surface changes to their appearance.

Making Choices Freely

For all of us, Susan Kano, a diet and nutrition expert, advises: "Ask yourself: am I making this choice freely, or am I feeling compelled to pursue approval and security [from others and myself] at all costs? Am I evaluating the situation and carefully choosing my actions, or am I doing what is expected without reference to my own judgment? Do I respect my own path, or am I 'putting up with it' because I feel unable to do otherwise? We will not like ourselves (or make the best possible decisions) if we are feeling *compelled* by a need for recognition and approval, or by a fear of failure."[9] For Christians, we can ask these questions with the Holy Spirit's assistance, yet He never abolishes our self-efficacy: our ability to make decisions and choose courses of action.

By way of example (and by no means meant to dictate each woman's need to think and pray through her own choices), the following actions might be some of the ways we free ourselves from body and appearance obsession. They comprise a combined list for those who might be too preoccupied with their appearance, or those who've felt themselves unworthy of much grooming at all. And again, I'm working on many of these myself.

- Accepting a current body weight.
- Believing we are worthy of taking care of our bodies.
- Buying clothing out of need, rather than merely wanting more.
- Considering carefully and prayerfully the motives behind a desire for plastic surgery.
- Dressing for a pleasant rather than a flashy look.
- Exercising at a reasonable level for good health, and letting go of body sculpting.
- Finding a general cleansing and makeup routine that works well and quickly, ceasing to search for more of the latest products.
- Giving up on worrying about cellulite.

- Grooming for cleanliness and presentability, not out of pride or competition.
- Investing in electrolysis so less time is spent "plucking."
- Jumping off the dieting merry-go-round and learning to eat healthily.
- Making appointments for regular dental and medical checkups.
- Monitoring the time and money spent on beauty services.
- Refusing to criticize other people's appearance or pushing them to meet certain body image standards.
- Signing up for and sticking with therapy to resolve body issues.
- Stopping the search for the fountain of youth.
- Starting to exercise.

We can determine if these choices are right for us if we feel ourselves being released from body and appearance anxieties—when how we look increasingly ceases to be an "issue" and more and more, we're accepting of and happy to be who we are. We are no longer looking for the "solution" to make us appear perfect or gorgeous. We understand that beauty isn't the answer to life and its problems. We are free.

The Freedom to Love

Whatever questions we dare to ask, whatever methods and changes we decide upon, we can remember that other women's answers will not necessarily resemble ours. Setting ourselves free is an individual process. As we make our decisions, experiencing both mistakes and victories, we can offer compassion not only to ourselves, but also to others. We can embrace and live with women who decide differently than us, not needing to criticize and change them, not playing the voice of God in their lives.

"You, my [sisters], were called to be free. But do not use your freedom to indulge the sinful nature; rather, serve one another in love. The entire law is summed up in a single command: 'Love your neighbor as yourself.' So I say, live by the Spirit, and you will not gratify the desires of the sinful nature" (Gal. 3:13–15). Following this biblical advice, we can refuse to judge and openly love our spiritual sisters. And to do so, we need the inner power of the soul.

Chapter Seven

THE POWER OF SOUL

Letting beauty exude from the woman within.

Last year after sharing all evening with my friend, I fell into bed sobbing and asking the Lord, "Where are all the older women who are supposed to be teaching my special friend about godly living?"

He reminded me of Proverbs 31:30 which says, "Charm is deceptive and beauty is fleeting." He spoke to me so clearly in my heart and said, "Through the media, women—even Christian women—have been taught the charm that is deceptive and to concentrate too much on the beauty that is fleeting." I cried and cried that night, and I repented as I realized the truth of this.

There is another part of Proverbs 31:30 that says, "but a woman who fears the Lord is to be praised." The Lord loves His women so much and has laid out His excellent plan for their lives in His Word. My prayer since that night has been for God to inspire me and other women to fear Him more and more.

I pray that He will teach us not to have charm that is deceptive and not to concentrate too much on beauty that is fleeting, but that He will teach us to become women who have inner beauty, "the unfading beauty of a gentle and quiet spirit, which is of great worth in His sight" (1 Pet. 3:4).
            —Cathy Horning, Women's Ministry Leader

Years ago when hippies inhabited the earth I belonged to a group called *Ekklesia,* an unconventional church for college students and other young adults. Led by a former Baptist minister, we met in an aging, two-story house in an old neighborhood not only on Sundays, but at various planned and spontaneous gatherings throughout the week.

Ekklesia opened its doors to people from all walks of life, so at our services drug addicts and honor-roll students, motorcycle mamas and squeaky clean Christians sat side-by-side to worship and listen to Gene, our leader, teach from the Bible. Though I hadn't declared myself a writer yet, in my late teens I already was an observer, and when I attended our services and parties, I soaked in the diversity around me.

One woman in particular caught my attention. I don't recall her name, but I'll always remember her buoyant personality and how much she loved Jesus. She had abandoned a wild lifestyle to accept Christ, and her face radiated the proof of her spiritual transformation. On some days she glowed.

After several months of hanging around at *Ekklesia,* though, I noticed the beautiful young woman no longer attended our meetings. Asking around, someone explained she had abandoned faith and returned to her former ways. Not long after I bumped into her unexpectedly and felt taken back by her appearance. Her demeanor—formerly soft, appealing, and congenial—looked hard, angry, and haggard, as if losing her spiritual joy added years to her face. The difference startled me so much I can still visualize it more than twenty years later. It was a poignant lesson about how the inner heart affects the outer appearance.

A Fortune in Our Faces

An old cliché says a woman's fortune is in her face, and biblically this can be true. Often if the spiritual riches of knowing Christ permeates our souls; it emanates from the face, creating an unerasable beauty. Scriptures tell us that a wicked person hardens his face, but wisdom brightens the countenance and changes the appearance (Prov. 21:29; Eccl. 8:1, KJV). I believe this observation refers to spiritual wisdom, not from merely knowing about God and purposing to do the right things, but from truly experiencing Him.

In the Bible when people encountered the Lord, it affected their appearance. When Moses descended from the mountain after an intimate meeting with God, his face shone so brightly, he placed a veil over it so the people wouldn't be afraid (Exod. 34:29-35). A repentant King David said his transgressions had taken away the light of his eyes, and that hoping in and praising God would be the "help of his countenance" (Ps. 38:10). When the angels announced Christ's birth to the shepherds, the glory of the Lord shone around them (Luke 2:9). After Jesus ascended a mountain to talk with Moses and Elijah, his face "shone like the sun" and a voice from a bright cloud spoke to the three disciples standing nearby, saying, "This is my Son, whom I love; with him I am well pleased. Listen to him!" (Matt. 17:5). God stood among them, and His light invaded those who understood this and communed with Him.

We could chalk up these episodes to the miracles reserved for biblical times, but I've seen a glow on the countenances of today's followers of Christ, the ones determined to pursue and press into the heart of God. I've observed this certain beauty in members of my prayer team, women I've met at conferences and people of the clergy. It's emanated from God-fearing faces at churches and in homes, during quiet moments and amid the onslaught of unremitting tragedies. Unlike Moses, these people have not needed a veil to cover their faces. Their glow, though not as bright as his mountaintop brilliance, draws people near instead of scaring them away.

It sounds strange, but it's possible to know about God and still be unwilling to wade into the depths with Him, to actually experience the Holy. We can even mingle with devoted people of God, doing and saying what they do, but still miss out on the Maker Himself. At the Mount of Transfiguration, instead of bowing and soaking in the pure splendor, Peter babbled about building a memorial to Jesus, Moses, and Elijah, and the heavenly Father intervened as if to say, "Shut up and listen to my Son!" Even on their walk back down the mountain with Jesus, it's evident this select group of disciples hadn't comprehended what they had seen.

The practical theologian A.W. Tozer would say these men hadn't allowed God to sear their souls and "happen" to them. He explained:

> There is a knowledge beyond and above that furnished by observation; it is knowledge received by faith. Divine revelation through the inspired Scriptures offers data which lie altogether outside of and above the power of the mind to discover. The mind can make its deductions after it has received these data by faith, but it cannot find them by itself. If we ever come to know these things it must be by receiving as true a body of doctrine which we have no way of verifying. This is the knowledge of faith.
>
> There is yet a purer knowledge than this; it is knowledge by direct spiritual experience. About it there is an immediacy that places it beyond doubt. Since it was not acquired by reason operating on intellectual data, the possibility of error is eliminated. Through the indwelling Spirit the human spirit is brought into immediate contact with higher spiritual reality. It looks upon, tastes, feels, and sees the powers of the world to come and has a conscious encounter with God invisible.
>
> Let it be understood that such knowledge is experienced rather than acquired. [A person] knows God in the last irreducible meaning of the word *know*. It may almost be said that God *happened to him*.[1]

Letting God Happen to Us

Tozer coined it well. Unless we let God "happen to us," we can't truly know Him. And without experiencing Him, we'll miss out on the inner beauty He can cultivate within us—an attractiveness that transcends the world's definition of beauty.

But how do we let God happen to us? How do we obtain this beauty?

Author Karen Burton Mains explains that when many people ask this question, they "don't particularly want a sincere answer; they want some sort of intellectual hocus-pocus, some kind of theorizing that sounds mystical and otherworldly. So the most offensive answer to give these people is: 'Read your Bible and pray, and ask for the Holy Spirit to teach you.' In their hearts, [Christians] already know what to do. It is often simply doing the things we already know to do."[2] We can't sidestep experiencing God for ourselves, by ourselves. And reading God's Word, spending time in prayer and listening for the Holy Spirit's prompting sets us on the path toward experiencing Him personally.

James told the early Christians, "Come near to God, and God will come near to you" (James 4:8). When we consistently and persistently draw close to God, He "happens" to us. Contrary to popular belief, a life-changing relationship requires that we spend both *quality* and *quantity* of time with the other person. It's also true with God. I know it sounds simple, but think about it: If we spent as much or more time with God than we do worrying about our appearance and searching out solutions to look more appealing, a miracle could happen. God could transform us into women of inner beauty, and this loveliness would seep into our faces.

I'm not advocating that we abandon caring for our bodies and appearance, but that we avoid substituting external props for God and His supernatural power. While we sit with the Father, we soak in His character and gather the faith to leap into His mystical kingdom. We begin to believe and trust that He can change us on the inside, rather than depending on mere mortals and their finite resources. We know Him well enough to ask for the miraculous power of living from the soul.

When we draw close to God, we eventually begin to experience rather than just know about Him. And we're gradually set free from the world's expectations.

But what about the *Ekklesia* woman whose joyful face hardened? Why did she abandon God and let her spiritual beauty fade? In her case I don't know the answer, and I hope that her decision was only temporary. Nevertheless, in my own experience I've learned that our level of commitment affects not only the staying power of our hearts, but also the "glowing power" on our faces.

Seed That Falls on Rock

Stephanie was a new Christian and although I didn't know her well, she seemed fun-loving and eager to learn. One night at a Bible study she asked me if I'd mentor her spiritually. Her enthusiasm enveloped me and without thinking I said yes.

The evening of our first study time together I hurriedly finished washing dishes before she arrived. With hands immersed in water, the New Testament parable of the sower popped into my head and with each additional swipe of a dish, the story pieced together and wouldn't leave. The biblical account is as follows:

While a large crowd was gathering and people were coming to Jesus from town after town, he told this parable:

"A farmer went out to sow his seed. As he was scattering the seed, some fell along the path; it was trampled on, and the birds of the air ate it up.

"Some fell on rock, and when it came up, the plants withered because they had no moisture.

"Other seed fell among thorns, which grew up with it and choked the plants.

"Still other seed fell on good soil. It came up and yielded a crop, a hundred times more than was sown." When he said this, he called out, "He who has ears to hear, let him hear."

His disciples asked him what this parable meant.

He said, "The knowledge of the secrets of the kingdom of God has been given to you, but to others I speak in parables, so that, 'though seeing, they may not see; though hearing, they may not understand.'

"This is the meaning of the parable: The seed is the word of God.

"Those along the path are the ones who hear, and then the devil comes and takes away the word from their hearts, so that they may not believe and be saved.

"Those on the rock are the ones who

receive the word with joy when they hear it, but they have no root. They believe for a while, but in the time of testing they fall away.

"The seed that fell among thorns stands for those who hear, but as they go on their way they are choked by life's worries, riches and pleasures, and they do not mature.

"But the seed on good soil stands for those with a noble and good heart, who hear the word, retain it, and by persevering produce a crop.

"No one lights a lamp and hides it in a jar or puts it under a bed. Instead, he puts it on a stand, so that those who come in can see the light" (Luke 8:4-13).

"Okay, Lord," I sighed. "If you want me to share this parable with Stephanie, I will. But I don't understand why."

After settling on the couch and chatting awhile, I told Stephanie we would begin by reading a parable from the book of Luke, chapter eight. Her face paled when I read, "Some fell on rock, and when it came up, the plants withered because they had no moisture" (v. 6). When I finished, Stephanie stammered, "I think I'm the seed on the rock." I assured her she could become a seed falling on good ground that "yielded a crop, a hundred times more than was sown" (v. 8) and told her how to grow as a Christian.

The next week Stephanie jilted our scheduled time together. She didn't respond to my phone messages, and I never heard from her again. I suspect when

Stephanie discovered Christianity required commitment, she decided it wasn't worth it.

When I think of Stephanie's change of mind, I can't help but evaluate myself. I'm still a Christian, while who-knows-what happened to her, but I realize how easily I can warm up to God when I need Him—and how swiftly I can draw back after He's granted my requests. I too soon forget that a relationship with God necessitates a two-way commitment. God saves us from sin and changes us because He loves us, but not so we can squander it on ourselves. Once we've received His grace, He asks us to multiply it a hundredfold in the lives of others.

We change and in turn, we help to change others. Bible teacher Hannah Whithall Smith explained this spiritual exchange:

> Many people think that the only thing proposed in religion is to improve the "old man," that is, the flesh; and that the way to do this is to discipline and punish it until it is compelled to behave. Hence comes the asceticism of the Buddhist and others; and hence, also, comes the idea that the "cross" for Christians consists in the painful struggles of this helpless "old man" to do the will of God, a will which in the very nature of things the flesh cannot understand or love.
> But a true comprehension of the religion of Christ shows us that what is really meant is the death of this old man and the birth in us of a "new creature," begotten of God, whose tastes and instincts are all in harmony

with God, *and to whom the doing of God's will must be, and cannot help being, a joy and a delight.*

It is not the old man thwarted and made miserable, by being compelled to submit to a will it dislikes, but is a new man, "created in Christ Jesus unto good works," and therefore doing these good works with ease and pleasure; a new nature, of divine origin, which is in harmony with the divine will, and therefore delights to do it.[3]

With this understanding we can say with the psalmist, "I desire to do your will, O my God; your law is within my heart" (Ps. 40:8). We can desire the inner beauty of the soul. Yet making a permanent commitment to God through Christ and reaching out to others isn't the whole story. God asks that we submit to His transformation of our character, and this requires further steps of surrender.

Surrendering All to God

For the past two years I've developed a devotional series called *Life Messages of Great Christians.* As I've worked with a publisher on selecting authors for this series, we've looked for people of the past who walked closely with God and left behind a body of printed work. With reverence I've gleaned from the writings of incomparable Christians like Amy Carmichael, Oswald Chambers, Andrew Murray, Charles Spurgeon, Corrie ten Boom, and more, posthumously creating a devotional from each of them.

While compiling and editing the fourth book, I began to discern a similar theme running through all of these formidable people's works. Though they didn't know one another and each articulated the theme in a unique style, these writers claimed that to walk with God in a way that transforms our character and releases spiritual power in our lives, we must surrender everything to Him. Some people completely surrender at the point of conversion, but with most of us, God works in stages until we lay down our own plans and desires and replace them with His. Bit by bit, sin by sin, habit by habit, attitude by attitude, stronghold by stronghold,[4] He asks us to surrender.

Read what these great Christians said about various aspects of surrender:

> *Amy Carmichael, missionary to India and ministry founder:* One morning I woke with these words on my lips: "We follow a stripped and crucified Savior."
>
> Those words go very deep. They touch everything, one's outer life as well as one's inner; motives, purposes, decisions, everything. Let them be with you. [You are] sure to have tests as well as many an unexpected joy. But if you follow a stripped and crucified Savior, and by the power of His resurrection seek to enter into the fellowship of His sufferings, you will go on in peace and be one of those blessed ones who spread peace all around.[5]
>
> *Oswald Chambers, Bible teacher and pastor to troops in Egypt:* When we are young in

grace we go where we want to go, but a time comes when Jesus says "another shall gird thee," and our will and wish is not asked for. This stage of spiritual experience brings us into fellowship with the Spirit of Jesus, for it is written large over His life that "even Christ pleased not Himself."

There is a distinct period in our experience when we cease to say, 'Lord show me Thy will,' and the realization begins to dawn that we are God's will, and He can do with us what He likes. We wake up to the knowledge that we have the privilege of giving ourselves over to God's will. It is a question of being yielded to God.[6]

Andrew Murray, missionary to South Africa: The life of absolute surrender is unfeigned obedience to God, fellowship with God in His Word, and prayer. Such life has two sides: absolute surrender to do what God wants us to do, and letting God work what He wants to do.

To do what God wants us to do, we must give up ourselves absolutely to the will of God. We must say absolutely to the Lord God: "By your grace I desire to do Your will in everything, every moment of every day."

Someone might ask, "Do you think that possible?" I reply, "What has God promised you? And what can God do to fill a vessel absolutely surrendered to Him?"

God wants to bless us in a way beyond

what we expect. From the beginning, ear has not heard nor has eye seen what God has prepared for them that wait for Him (1 Cor. 2:9).[7]

Charles Spurgeon, renowned British preacher: [People who have surrendered all to God] have seen a world of iniquity hidden in a single act, or thought, or imagination of sin; and they have avoided it with horror—have passed by and would have nothing to do with it. But if the straight road to heaven be through flames, through floods, through death itself, they had sooner go through all these torments than turn one inch aside to tread an easy and an erroneous path.

I say this should help us when Satan tempts us to commit little sins—this should help us to the answer, "No, Satan, if God's people think it great, they are true. I must shun all sin, even though you say it is but little."[8]

Corrie ten Boom, Nazi prison camp survivor and worldwide speaker: Denying ourselves, taking up our crosses, and following Jesus is not like jumping from an airplane towards earth with parachutes on our backs. It means being safe in the hands of Jesus, yoke-fellows with Him. His joy in us, and our joy fulfilled.

When we trust ourselves we are doing the wrong thing. We can fall into the error of pride on the one hand, or discouragement on the other. We are really strong when we are weak; weak when we are strong. So following in the footsteps of Jesus, taking the steps— yes, and the jumps into the unknown, we can become paratroopers. We can storm the enemy's territory and win souls for Jesus. But only if we obey.[9]

Struggling to Surrender

For many years I've struggled against the idea of absolute surrender, thinking it frightening and unfair, as if God couldn't be trusted with my total life. Didn't He have enough already? But particularly in the last few years, as God has lovingly and persistently shed His light on each thing I cling to, I've grown to understand that surrender is not a punishment, but the gateway to joy. It sets us on a path filled with God's spiritual blessings.

Andrew Murray explained, "God has prepared unheard-of things, things we never can think of— blessings, much more wonderful than we can imagine, more mighty than we can conceive. They are divine blessings. We must come at once and say, 'I give myself absolutely to God, to His will, to do only what God wants.' It is God who will enable us to carry out the surrender."[10] And Corrie ten Boom asked and answered, "What is total surrender? A joyful experience."[11]

I've discovered, too, that when the Master brings us to surrender, our hearts are melted and our eyes are opened so with relief we say, "Yes, Lord, I understand it now. I'll give this up. It's hurting me and you want to heal and free me." We finally comprehend that we're surrendering to a lover, not to a dictator. Unfortunately, before we understand this, many of us run away, believing there is nothing better than what we clutch in our hands. And what we cling to gradually destroys us.

It may seem out of place to discuss spiritual surrender in a book about bodies and beauty, but if we're to lay every area of our lives at God's throne, then our desire for physical perfection belongs there too. When we surrender ourselves to God, He begins replacing the world's definition of attractiveness with the loveliness of His indwelling Spirit.

The Inner Qualities of Beauty

A few weeks ago at a conference a woman said to me, "You have such a gentle spirit." I was so surprised I wanted to look around for my mother. I've always considered Mom a gentle soul, and I've loved her for it, but never thought that quality would describe me. Especially in work situations, I've been more the assertive, pushy type.

"Who, me?" I answered awkwardly, and if that woman happens to read this book I'm openly apologizing to her. I should have said, "thank you."

A few weeks later at a friend's house she said to me, "Judy, there's a real gentleness about you these days," and she meant it as a compliment. Naomi has seen me at my worst and I couldn't slough off her observation. On the drive home I thought, *Well, maybe I'm finally letting God shine through.* I hadn't been aware of this "gentling," but that is how God works: as we obey what He's telling us, He decorates our character with spiritual beauty.

As God has taught me about surrender, He repeatedly has asked me to relinquish the things I think are best for me—the things that give me identity—and replace them with His purposes and character traits. He's spotlighted how I've patterned my character after the world's standards rather than His, and perhaps that's why I've had to adjust to being called gentle. In the world's eyes, especially in the business world, gentleness is often thought of as wimpy, but God says "the unfading beauty of a gentle and quiet spirit . . . is of great worth in God's sight" (1 Pet. 3:4). Gentleness is one of the fruits of the Holy Spirit.

Believe me, I still have plenty of character dysfunctions that need God's touch, but He promises if I keep surrendering to Him, they'll be replaced with the fruit of His Spirit. These fruit are the qualities of inner beauty: love, joy, peace, patience, kindness, goodness, faithfulness, gentleness, and self-control (Gal. 5:22). Paul reminded believers that, "Those who belong to Christ Jesus have crucified the sinful nature with its passions and desires," and this is how "we live by the Spirit, . . . keep in step with the Spirit" and cultivate the fruit of the Spirit in our lives (vv. 24-25).

The Scriptures also indicate how these qualities of inner beauty affect the way we live and relate to others. For example:

- *Love.* "A new command I give you: Love one another. As I have loved you, so you must love one another. By this all men will know that you are my disciples, if you love one another" (John 13:34-35). "Now that you have purified yourselves by obeying the truth so that you have sincere love for your brothers, love one another deeply, from the heart" (1 Pet. 1:22).

- *Joy.* "You have loved righteousness and hated wickedness; therefore God, your God, has set you above your companions by anointing you with the oil of joy" (Heb. 1:9). "Consider it pure joy, my brothers, whenever you face trials of many kinds, because you know that the testing of your faith develops perseverance. Perseverance must finish its work so that you may be mature and complete, not lacking anything" (James 1:2-4).

- *Peace.* "Do not be anxious about anything, but in everything, by prayer and petition, with thanksgiving, present your requests to God. And the peace of God, which transcends all understanding, will guard your hearts and your minds in Christ Jesus" (Phil. 4:6-7). "Peace I leave with you; my peace I give you. I do not give to you as the world gives. Do not let your hearts be troubled and do not be afraid" (John 14:27).

- *Patience.* "A hot-tempered man stirs up dissension, but a patient man calms a quarrel" (Prov. 15:18). "Be completely humble and gentle; be patient, bearing with one another in love. Make every effort to keep the unity of the Spirit through the bond of peace" (Eph. 4:2).

- *Kindness:* "Therefore, as God's chosen people, holy and dearly loved, clothe yourselves with compassion, kindness, humility, gentleness and patience" (Col. 3:12). "Be kind and compassionate to one another, forgiving each other, just as in Christ God forgave you" (Eph. 4:32).

- *Goodness.* "Surely goodness and love will follow me all the days of my life, and I will dwell in the house of the Lord forever" (Ps. 23:6). "I myself am convinced, my brothers, that you yourselves are full of goodness, complete in knowledge and competent to instruct one another" (Rom. 15:14).

- *Faithfulness.* "Now fear the Lord and serve him with all faithfulness" (Josh. 24:14). "It gave me great joy to have some brothers come and tell about your faithfulness to the truth and how you continue to walk in the truth" (3 John 3).

- *Gentleness.* "Let your gentleness be evident to all. The Lord is near" (Phil. 4:5). "Always be prepared to give an answer to everyone who asks you to give the reason for the hope that you have. But do this with gentleness and respect" (1 Pet. 3:15).

- *Self-control.* "He who heeds discipline shows the way to life, but whoever ignores correction leads others astray" (Prov. 10:17). "For this very reason, make every effort to add to your faith goodness; and to goodness, knowledge; and to knowledge, self-control" (2 Pet. 1:5-6).

If we gave up fussing and complaining about our looks and began expressing the fruit of the Spirit, we'd be remarkable women indeed. The question is: How many of us are willing to surrender and bear Christ's image?

Choosing Whom to Serve

Lest we become overwhelmed by this list of spiritual attributes, we can remember that God melds these characteristics into us over time, and often one at a time. Plus, we don't cultivate and exude inner beauty with our own strength, but through the Holy Spirit's power. The Apostle Peter said, "His divine power has given us everything we need for life and godliness through our knowledge of him who called us by his own glory and goodness. Through these he has given us his very great and precious promises, so that through them you may participate in the divine nature and escape the corruption in the world caused by evil desires" (2 Pet. 1:3–4).

Then Peter reminds us that spiritual growth is an adding-on rather than an all-at-once process: "For this very reason, make every effort to add to your faith goodness; and to goodness, knowledge; and to knowledge, self-control; and to self-control, perseverance; and to perseverance, godliness; and to godliness, brotherly kindness; and to brotherly kindness, love. For if you possess these qualities in increasing measure, they will keep you from being ineffective and unproductive in your knowledge of our Lord Jesus Christ" (2 Pet. 1:5–8). Once the fruit of the Spirit shine from us, they tend to operate in clusters rather than singularly, but the overall "package" causes people to notice because we're walking in truth and freedom. Even though the world tries to discredit the Spirit's qualities, spiritual seekers feel drawn to the "aroma of Christ" within us (2 Cor. 2:15), for He is the essence of true beauty.

Yet it's still our decision as to whether God can cultivate His glorious beauty in us. Even if we've uncovered our family's and culture's influences on us; if we've learned that in God's eyes our physical appearance is beautiful; if we've considered how to be less obsessive about our looks, we still need to choose whether we'll surrender to God and His transforming power or continue wallowing in body and beauty worries. Joshua challenged a wavering people by saying, "But if serving the Lord seems undesirable to you, then choose for yourselves this day whom you will serve, whether the gods your forefathers served beyond the River, or the gods of the Amorites, in whose land you are living. But as for me and my household, we will serve the Lord" (Josh. 24:15).

Whomever we choose to serve—the gods of external beauty or the God of internal beauty—it affects all of ourselves, all of our lives. It is my hope that in how we look, why we act, and what we choose, we will serve the Lord.

Afterword
HEALTHY, WEALTHY AND WISE

Developing a process for change.

You have a right—and a responsibility—to judge yourself according to realistic standards. A right to feel comfortable in your own skin.

It's possible to reduce preoccupation with appearance, to break destructive habits, and to find more constructive alternatives. But knowing what to do is not enough. Doing is essential. So start somewhere.

In the end, self-esteem comes through personal development—through becoming a competent and caring human being. By transforming your image from within, you can move beyond body loathing toward bodylove.

—Rita Freedman, Psychologist

Question: How many psychologists does it take to change a lightbulb? *Answer:* Only one. But the lightbulb has to want to change.

It's a corny joke, but deep truth lies within it. If we don't want to change, be it our attitudes or habits or lifestyle, no amount of help from books or tapes or seminars or therapists will budge us. And because God gave humanity a free will, not even He can transform us unless we give Him the permission.

But if we really desire change, if we unquestionably want release from our bondages, then with the supernatural power of the Holy Spirit, we can change from the inside out. We can choose to let go of a preoccupation with our appearance. We can walk in freedom, becoming spiritually healthy, wealthy, and wise.

Still, the responsibility to change rests on each woman's shoulders; no one else can do the work for us. Accordingly, as I've worked on this book I've wrestled with the questions, "How much can I do to help women work through a negative body image? How much do women need to work through on their own?" I decided that as a writer I can research the body image dilemma, tell parts of my own story, offer my observations, and teach what God says about appearance and surrendering to Him. But as much as I'd like to ensure that my readers release themselves from appearance anxieties, I can't do the work for them.

So this is where my work ends and yours begins. If you want to change your attitudes about body image and appearance, whether they be small alterations or big transformations, it's up to you. You can begin by working through the principles in this book, and then obtain additional resources that apply specifically to your needs. For example, you may need to enter into counseling with an experienced therapist who specializes in body-image problems. Or you might want to read additional books about appearance anxieties, working through body-image experts' step-by-step processes for change. (See the bibliography.) You could conduct an in-depth Bible study on the topics of beauty and/or God's love for you. Or you may benefit from a Bible study or support group. You may find release by working through the beauty issue on your own; you may need the encouragement of one confidant or various people. Or you may want to do all of these ideas, mapping out a plan for your unique process. (The worksheet on pages 158–161 can help you begin.) The goal is to begin changing bit by bit, day by day, until you are free.

Whatever the case, it's important to begin doing something, and it's crucial that these activities be guided by God rather than man. You can pray to Him, "Show me your ways, O Lord, teach me your paths; guide me in your truth and teach me, for you are God my Savior, and my hope is in you all day long" (Ps. 25:4–5). And He will answer, "Whether you turn to the right or to the left, your ears will hear a voice behind you, saying, 'This is the way; walk in it'" (Is. 30:21).

PASSAGE TO FREEDOM

Releasing yourself from appearance anxieties.

By making a copy of these pages or marking in this book, think through and write out a strategy for releasing yourself from a preoccupation with your body and appearance. Sign and date this plan, and share it with someone who will lovingly help you accomplish it.

Questions to Consider

1. What influencers have affected my opinion of my appearance? How?

2. How can I forgive and be free from these influencers?

3. What body/beauty issues do I need to work through?

4. How can I work through these issues?

5. How can I embrace that God loves and accepts who I am?

6. How can I protect the progress I make?

7. How can I respond to those who criticize or pressure me about my appearance?

8. What changes do I need to make in my grooming, exercise, or other body-related habits?

9. How can I develop a healthy lifestyle?

10. How can I continue to surrender my body image to God?

A Personal Strategy

These are the steps I will take to free myself from a preoccupation with my body and appearance:

-
-
-
-
-
-
-
-

Date:

Signed:

QUESTIONS

Use these questions in a group or individual setting to clarify your responses to each chapter in this book.

Introduction: The Unbeautiful Me

1. Why were you interested in reading *The Woman Behind the Mirror*?
2. What aspects of body image do you struggle with?
3. At this point do you know why you struggle with these body image issues?
4. Who can you ask to support you while dealing with the topics in this book?
5. How can you commit the reading/study of this book to God, asking for His insight and assistance?

Chapter One: Mirror Images

1. What opinions about appearance do you still carry from your childhood or youth?
2. Why have these opinions stayed with you?
3. How have you tried to compensate for your feelings about your appearance?
4. Do you relate to any of our culture's appearance obsessions mentioned in this chapter? If so, which ones?
5. What do you like about your appearance? What do you dislike? Why?

Chapter Two: All in the Family

1. To fit into your family system, what beliefs have you adopted about appearance?

2. Specifically, what did your mother teach you about a woman's appearance? How have you responded to her opinions?

3. Specifically, what did your father teach you about a woman's appearance? How have you responded to his opinions?

4. How have siblings affected your body image? Why?

5. Did anyone in your family, through emotional or physical abuse, affect your opinions about your body/appearance? If so, how?

Chapter Three: The Beauty Trap

1. How did (do) puberty and peers shape your body image?

2. How much do you allow male opinions to affect your opinion of your appearance? Why?

3. How does the media's influence affect your body image? How often do you allow the media to influence you?

4. Do you feel the pressure of the beauty imperative on the job? Why, or why not?

5. Have you ever struggled with the pain of disabilities or pornography, either yours or someone else's? Has this affected your body image? If so, how?

6. How do you feel about aging's effects on your body? Why?

Chapter Four: Reflections of Eve

1. How have your opinions of beauty changed during your lifetime? What or who has influenced these changes?

2. Looking at yourself, how can you tell you were created in God's image?

3. How would you like people to respect the way God uniquely made you?

4. Do you view God as redemptive or punitive? How does this viewpoint affect your body image?

5. Do you believe God cares about how you look? Why, or why not?

Chapter Five: Making Peace with Pressure

1. Who or what pressures you to be concerned about your appearance? How do you feel about this pressure?

2. What lies have you believed about your appearance?

3. Do you think your perception of your body is accurate? Why, or why not?

4. Do you have conscious or unconscious needs to hang on to a poor opinion of yourself? Why, or why not?

5. How can you begin telling yourself the truth about your body/appearance?

6. What do you need to grieve about your body beliefs?

7. How can you protect your desire to free yourself from worrying about appearances?

8. Whose negative opinions about your body do you encounter? How can you respond to them?

Chapter Six: The Art of Change

1. Have you been wrapped up in pride about your appearance? If so, how?

2. How do you feel about God's hatred of pride?

3. What is your definition of stewardship as it applies to your body?

4. How can you gauge the difference between pride and stewardship?

5. How can you implement a humble and balanced approach to body care into your life? What will you need to accept about yourself? What will you need to change? Why?

Chapter Seven: The Power of Soul

1. Have you made beauty issues more important than spiritual growth? Explain.

2. What aspects of spiritual growth do you need to explore and practice?

3. Are any of the Spirit's fruit evident in your life? Explain.

4. How can you renew or increase your desire for God?

5. How do/will you know that you have inner beauty?

6. If there is no "power of soul" in your life, do you want it? If so, how can you gain it?

Afterword: Healthy, Wealthy, and Wise

1. How can you ensure you're following a healthy lifestyle?

2. How can you pursue spiritual wealth in your life?

3. Specifically, what wisdom do you need to apply to your body attitudes?

4. If you could remember only one principle from this book, what would it be?

5. Today, how can you begin living the spiritual principles presented in this book?

6. What further information about body image do you need beyond this book? How can you begin this exploration?

NOTES

Chapter One: Mirror Images

1. "Body Mania" by Judith Rodin, Ph.D., *Psychology Today*, January/February, 1992, 56.

2. "Adolescent Appearance and Self-Concept" by Kathleen E. Musa, Ph.D. and Mary Ellen Roach, Ph.D., *Adolescence*, Fall 1973, 385. "Body Image," by Ellen Berscheid, Elaine Walster and George Bohrnstedt, *Psychology Today*, November 1972, 119. "Body Love, Body Hate" by Marianne Wait, *Ladies Home Journal*, January 1992, 30. "Body Mania" by Judith Rodin, Ph.D., *Psychology Today*, January/February, 1992, 56 "Dieting: The Losing Game" by Anastasia Toufexis, *Time*, January 20, 1986, 54. "Mission Impossible" by Karen S. Schneider, *People Weekly*, June 3, 1996, 64. "Pumping Irony" by Martha Brant, *Newsweek*, October 23, 1995, 88. "The Great American Shape-Up" by Thomas F. Cash, Barbara A. Winstead and Louis H. Janda, *Psychology Today*, April 1986, 30.

3. "Feeling Fat in a Thin Society" by the Editors, *Glamour*, February 1984, 198.

4. "Do I Look Fat?" by Neala S. Schwartzberg, *Parents*, January 1990, 66.

5. "Thigh Anxiety?" by Dana Points, *Mademoiselle*, May 1996, 150.

6. "The Littlest Dieters" by Boeth Donovan, Marianna Goswell, Nadine Joseph and Jean Seligmann, *Newsweek*, July 27, 1987, 48.

7. "Images of Women: Should We All Look Like Kate?" by Todd Olson, *Scholastic Update*, March 8, 1996, 128.

8. "Some Body to Love" by Stephanie Dolgoff, *Longevity*, December 1994, n.p.

9. "The Bad Body Blues" by Cheryl Sacra, *Women's Sports and Fitness*, April 1994, 66.

10. Schwartzberg, 66.

11. "Eating Disorders" by Richard L. Worsnop, *CQ Researcher*, December 18, 1992, 1099.

12. "Portrait of an Obsession" by Barbara Hey, *Health*, June 1991, 68.

13. "Body Wars" by Andrew Kimbrell, *Utne Reader*, May/June 1992, 52.

14. Patricia Fallon, Melanie A. Katzman and Susan C. Wooley, *Feminist Perspectives on Eating Disorders* (New York: The Guilford Press, 1994), 342.

15. "Up Close with Naomi Wolf" by Daryn Eller, *Health*, June 1991, 71.

Chapter Two: All in the Family

1. Judi Hollis, *Fat Is a Family Affair* (New York: HarperCollins Publishers, 1985), 9.

2. Colette Dowling, *Perfect Women: Hidden Feelings of Inadequacy and the Drive to Perform* (New York: Summit Books, 1988), 24-25.

3. "Daughters of Dieters" by Anne Taylor Fleming, *Glamour*, November 1994, 222.

4. Joni E. Johnston, Psy. D., *Appearance Obsession: Learning to Love the Way You Look* (Deerfield Beach, FL: Health Communications, Inc., 1994), 5.

5. Carolynn Hillman, C. S. W., *Love Your Looks: How to Stop Criticizing and Start Appreciating Your Appearance* (New York: Simon & Schuster, 1996), 72.

6. David Blankenhorn, *Fatherless America: Confronting Our Most Urgent Social Problem* (New York: HarperCollins, 1995), 1. He cites Larry L. Bumpass, "Children and Marital Disruption: A Replication and Update," *Demography*, 21, No. 1 (February 1984), 72-82; James A. Sweet, "Children's Experience in Single-Parent Families: Implications of Cohabitation and Marital Transitions," *Family Planning Perspectives*, 21, no. 6 (November/December 1989), 256-60; Frank F. Furstenberg, Jr., and Andrew J. Cherlin, *Divided Families: What Happens to Children When Parents Part* (Cambridge, Mass: Harvard University Press, 1991), 11.

7. Hillman, 69.

8. Johnston, 50.

9. Nancy Friday, *The Power of Beauty* (New York: HarperCollins Publishers, 1996), 79. (Although I do not endorse Nancy Friday's

lifestyle, some of her writings, or her opinions about sex, she does offer interesting insights into female relationships.)

10. Hillman, 74.

11. Hillman, 75.

Chapter Three: The Beauty Trap

1. Johnston, 61-62.

2. Mary Pipher, Ph.D., *Reviving Ophelia: Saving the Lives of Adolescent Girls* (New York: Ballantine Books, 1994), 184-185. Also see "Toward an Understanding of Risk Factors for Bulimia" by Ruth H. Striegel-Moore, Lisa R. Silberstein and Judith Rodin, *American Psychologist*, March 1986, 246, and "Cultural Expectations of Thinness in Women" by David M. Garner, Paul E. Garfinkel, Donald Schwartz and Michael Thompson, *Psychological Reports*, October 1980, 483.

3. "The Incentive Value of Physical Attractiveness for Young Children" by Karen K. Dion, *Personality and Social Psychology Bulletin*, Winter 1977, 67, and Pipher, 184.

4. Pipher, 184.

5. "Beauty Is Talent" by David Landy and Harold Sigall, *Journal of Personality and Social Psychology*, March 1974, 299. Also Pipher, 184.

6. Pipher, 184.

7. This phrase derives from "What Is Beautiful Is Good" by Ellen Berscheid, Karen Dion and Elaine Walster, *Journal of Personality and Social Psychology*, October 1972, 285. Also see "When Beauty May Fail" by Marshall Dermer and Darrel L. Thiel, *Journal of Personality and Social Psychology*, June 1975, 1168, and "Physical Attractiveness" by Ellen Berscheid and Elaine Walster, *Advances in Experimental Social Psychology* (New York: Academic Press, 1974), 199.

8. Marion Crook, B.Sc.N., *The Body Image Trap: Understanding and Rejecting Body Image Myths* (North Vancouver, British Columbia: International Self-Counsel Press Ltd., 1991), 14.

9. "Gender Differences in Concern with Body Weight and Physical Appearance Over the Life Span" by Shelly Chaiken, Gordon L. Fleet and Patricia Pliner, *Personality and Social Psychology Bulletin*, June 1990, 263. "Socioeconomic Status and Obesity: A

Review of the Literature" by Jeffrey Sobal and Albert J. Stunkard, *Psychological Bulletin*, March 1989, 260.

10. "Physcial Attractiveness, Social Relations, and Personality Style" by Dennis Krebs and Allen A. Adinolfi, *Journal of Personality and Social Psychology*, February 1975, 250.

11. "Somatic Attractiveness: As In Other Things, Moderation Is Best" by Harvey R. Freeman, *Psychology of Women Quarterly*, September 1985, 311.

12. "Gender Differences in Effects of Physical Attractiveness on Romantic Attraction: A Comparison Across Five Research Paradigms" by Alan Feingold, *Journal of Personality and Social Psychology*, November 1990, 981. "Gender and Ethnic Differences in Obesity-Related Behaviors and Attitudes in a College Sample" by Mary B. Harris and Laurie C. Walters, *Journal of Applied Social Psychology*, October 1-15, 1991, 1545.

13. "Body Image, Attitudes to Weight, and Misperceptions of Figure Preferences of the Opposite Sex: A Comparison of Men and Women in Two Generations" by April Fallon and Paul Rozin, *Journal of Abnormal Psychology*, August 1988, 342. "Women and Weight: A Normative Discontent" by Judith Rodin, Lisa Silberstein and Ruth Striegel-Moore, *Nebraska Symposium on Motivation*, Volume 32, 1984, 267.

14. Friday, 174.

15. Michael Gross, *Model: The Ugly Business of Beautiful Women* (New York: Warner Books, 1995), 4.

16. "My Body, My Self" by Megan Othersen, *Runner's World*, June 1993, 68.

17. "The Body Game" by the Editors, *People Weekly*, January 11, 1993, 84.

18. "Mission Impossible" by Karen S. Schneider, *People Weekly*, June 5, 1996, 64.

19. "Panel Tracks Shifts in Women's Images" by Janet Ozzard, *Women's Wear Daily*, September 1995, 10. "Social Comparison and the Idealized Images of Advertising" by Marsha Richins, *Journal of Consumer Research*, June 1991, 71. "The Beauty Myth and Female Consumers" by Cynthia Hanson, Ronald Paul Hill and Debra Lynn Stephens, *Abstract from the American Council on Consumer Interests*, 1994, n.p.

20. "Beauty and the Bucks" by Barbara Rudolph, *Time*, October 7, 1991, 40.

21. Alexander Walker, *Audrey* (New York: St. Martin's Press, 1994), 262.

22. Schneider, 49.

23. Ibid., 49.

24. Naomi Wolf, *The Beauty Myth* (New York: Doubleday, 1991), 28.

25. Wolf, 35-40.

26. "Being Attractive, Advantage or Disadvantage? Performance-Based Evaluations and Recommended Personnel Actions as a Function of Appearance, Sex, and Job Type" by Madeline E. Heilman and Melanie H. Stopeck, *Organizational Behavior and Human Decision Processes*, April 1985, 202. "Attractiveness and Corporate Success: Different Casual Attributions for Males and Females" by Madeline E. Heilman and Melanie H. Stopeck, *Journal of Applied Psychology*, February 1985, 379. "The Eye of the Beholder" by Thomas F. Cash and Louis H. Janda, *Psychology Today*, December 1984, 46. "When Beauty Is Beastly: The Effects of Appearance and Sex on Evaluations of Job Applicants for Managerial and Nonmanagerial Jobs" by Madeline E. Heilman and Lois R. Saruwatari, *Organizational Behavior and Human Performance*, June 1979, 360.

27. Susan Wendell, *The Rejected Body* (New York: Routledge, 1966), 4.

28. "Why Women Pose in the Buff" by Rona Maynard, *Chatelaine*, January 1986, 57.

29. Maynard, 71.

30. "If Your Lover Uses Porn" by Carol Lynn Mithers, *Glamour*, November 1988, 274.

31. "Hers" by Kathy Pollitt, *The New York Times*, January 16, 1986, C2.

32. Friday, 74–75.

Chapter Four: Reflections of Eve

1. Dr. Miriam Stoppard, *Woman's Body: A Manual for Life* (New York: Dorling Kindersley Publishing, 1994), 18.

2. The examples used in this section are drawn from Crook, 26-33.

3. Wolf, 243.

4. Stoppard, 17.

5. Wolf, 243.

6. Clarissa Pinkola Estés, *Women Who Run with the Wolves* (New York: Ballantine Books, 1992), 202-203. Although I do not endorse Estés' spiritual philosophy, she makes a good point about how we long for people to accept our appearance.

7. Estés, 203.

8. Lawrence O. Richards, *Expository Dictionary of Bible Words* (Zondervan Publishing House, 1985), 315-316.

9. *The NIV Study Notes for Macintosh* (Grand Rapids: Zondervan Publishing House, 1991), 1.

10. Madeleine L'Engle, *And It Was Good* (Harold Shaw Publishers, 1983), 58.

11. Edith Schaeffer, *Lifelines: God's Framework for Christian Living* (Westchester, IL: Crossway Books, 1982), 19.

12. "Perfect Match: Do Ideal Mates Come in Symmetrical Packages?" by Elizabeth Pennisi, *Science News*, January 28, 1995, 60.

13. In Genesis 4:1, when Eve gave birth to Cain, she called him a gift from the Lord. The same chapter tells of God's involvement with the couple's sons, Cain and Abel. From there, the entire Old Testament recounts God's relationship with humanity.

14. 2 Corinthians 4:6-7; Hebrews 5:8-9; 10:14; 11:39-40; 12:22-23.

15. In addition to reveling in human love, many theologians consider the Song of Solomon a metaphor for Christ's relationship with His bride, the Church. In this verse the bride (Christians) calls her loved one (Christ) "altogether lovely." If we are reflections of Christ, this description also applies to us.

16. Philippians 3:20-21; 1 Corinthians 15:51-53; 1 Thessalonians 5:23.

Chapter Five: Making Peace with Pressure

1. Adaptation of "The Emperor's New Clothes" by Hans Christian Andersen. For the original and complete story, see *Hans Christian Andersen: The Complete Fairy Tales and Stories*, edited by Erik Christian Haugaard (New York: Doubleday, 1974), 77-81.

2. John Bartlett, *Familiar Quotations* (Boston: Little, Brown and Company, 1980), 388.

3. "Larger Than Life" by J. Kevin Thompson, *Psychology Today*, April 1986, 42-44. "The Etiology of Adolescents' Perceptions of Their Weight" by Sharon M. Desmond, James H. Price, Nancy

Gray and Janelle K. O'Connell, *Journal of Youth and Adolescence*, December 1986, 472-473. "Mirror Images" by Cheryl Sacra, *Health*, March 1990, 72.

4. "Sex Differences in Perceptions of Desirable Body Shape" by April E. Fallon and Paul Rozin, *Journal of Abnormal Pscyhology*, February 1985, 102.

5. "Larger Than Life," 42.

6. Linda Tschirhart Sanford and Mary Ellen Donovan, *Women and Self-Esteem* (New York: Penguin Books USA, Inc., 1985), 407.

7. Paul Tournier, *The Meaning of Persons* (San Francisco: Harper & Row Publishers, 1957), 52.

8. M. Scott Peck, M.D., *The Road Less Traveled* (New York: Simon & Schuster, Inc., 1978), 44.

9. Jan Silvious, *Who's in Control?* (Chattanooga: Precept Ministries, 1997), 9-10.

10. Jane R. Hirschmann and Carol H. Munter, *When Women Stop Hating Their Bodies* (New York: Ballantine Books, 1985), 297.

11. Hirschmann and Hunter, 309.

12. Debra Evans, *Beauty and the Best* (Colorado Springs: Focus on the Family Publishing, 1993), 186.

13. *Circle of Friends*, Terence Clegg, executive producer, 102 minutes, HBO Savoy Films, 1995, videocassette.

14. Ingrid Trobisch, *The Confident Woman* (San Francisco: HarperSanFrancisco, 1993), 9.

Chapter Six: The Art of Change

1. Deuteronomy 11:26-28; 28:1-8; 30:8-10, 19-20.

2. Life Application Bible, New International Version (Wheaton, Ill. and Grand Rapids, Mich.: Tyndale House Publishers, Inc. and Zondervan Publishing House, 1991), 1174.

3. Stoppard, 15.

4. Stoppard, 37.

5. Information about the body's intricacies derives from Stoppard, 11-15, 27, 37.

6. Sophocles, "Antigone," *The Theban Plays* (New York: Penguin Books, 1947), n.p.

7. William Shakespeare, "Hamlet," Act Two, Scene Two. G. B. Harrison, editor, *Shakespeare: The Complete Works* (New York: Harcourt, Brace & World, Inc., 1968), 901.

8. Dr. Paul Brand and Philip Yancey, *In His Image* (Grand Rapids, Mich.: Zondervan Publishing House, 1984), 22-23.

9. Susan Kano, *Making Peace with Food* (New York: Harper & Row, Publishers, 1989), 98.

Chapter Seven: The Power of Soul

1. A. W. Tozer, *Man: The Dwelling Place of God* (Harrisburg, Pa: Christian Publications, Inc., 1966), 51–52.

2. "Warming Up" by Karen Burton Mains, *Sunday Digest*, January 13, 1985 (Elgin, Ill.: David C. Cook Publishing), 3.

3. Hannah Whitall Smith, *The Common Sense Teaching of the Bible* (Old Tappan, N.J.: Fleming H. Revell, 1985), 112–13.

4. If you sense that pride or body/beauty obsession may be a spiritual stronghold in your life, prayerfully read *The Adversary* by Mark I. Bubeck, published by Moody Press, Chicago, Ill., 1975. It is a helpful guide to breaking Satan's power and strongholds in a Christian's life.

5. Amy Carmichael, compiled by Judith Couchman, *A Very Present Help* (Ann Arbor, Mich.: Servant Publications, 1996), 72.

6. Oswald Chambers, compiled by Judith Couchman, *Growing Deeper with God* (Ann Arbor, Mich.: Servant Publications, 1997), n.p.

7. Andrew Murray, compiled by Judith Couchman, *Loving God with All Your Heart* (Ann Arbor, Mich.: Servant Publications, 1996), 104-105.

8. Charles Spurgeon, compiled by Judith Couchman, *For Me to Live Is Christ* (Ann Arbor, Mich.: Servant Publications, 1998), n.p.

9. Corrie ten Boom, compiled by Judith Couchman, *Anywhere He Leads Me* (Ann Arbor, Mich.: Servant Publications, 1997), n.p.

10. Murray, 105.

11. ten Boom, n.p.

BIBLIOGRAPHY

Although many of these books don't support a Christian viewpoint, they present additional ideas and practical advice related to the topics in *The Woman Behind the Mirror*. Read with discernment, these titles can assist women with releasing themselves from body and appearance obsession. Books marked with an asterisk (*) contain practical help for this process.

Aburdene, Patricia and Naisbitt, John. *Megatrends for Women*. New York: Villard Books, 1992.

*Atrens, Dale M. *Don't Diet*. New York: William Morrow and Company, 1988.

Blankenhorn, David. *Fatherless America: Confronting Our Most Urgent Problem*. New York: HarperCollins Publishers, 1995.

Brand, Paul and Yancey, Philip. *Fearfully and Wonderfully Made*. Grand Rapids: Zondervan Publishing House, 1980.

Brand, Paul and Yancey, Philip. *In His Image*. Grand Rapids: Zondervan Publishing House, 1984.

*Cash, Thomas. *What Do You See When You Look in the Mirror? Helping Yourself to a Positive Body Image*. New York: Bantam Books, 1995.

Cherin, Kim. *The Hungry Self: Women, Eating, and Identity*. New York: Random House, 1985.

Couchman, Judith. *Lord, Please Help Me to Change*. Dallas: Word Publishing, 1992.

*Crook, Marion. *The Body Image Trap: Understanding and Rejecting Body Image Myths*. North Vancouver: Self-Counsel Press, 1991.

Dowling, Colette. *Perfect Women: Hidden Fears of Inadequacy and the Drive to Perform*. New York: Summit Books, 1988.

Emme with Daniel Paisner. *True Beauty*. New York: G. P. Putnam, 1996.

Evans, Debra. *Beauty and the Best: A Christian Woman's Guide to True Beauty*. Colorado Springs: Focus on the Family Publishing, 1993.

*Freedman, Rita. *Bodylove: Learning to Like Our Looks and Ourselves*. New York: Harper & Row Publishers, 1988.

Grealy, Lucy. *Autobiography of a Face*. New York: Houghton Mifflin Company, 1994.

Gross, Michael. *Model: The Ugly Business of Beautiful Women*. New York: Time Warner Books, Inc., 1995.

Hakala, D'Orso. *Thin Is a Four-Letter Word*. Boston: Little, Brown and Company, 1996.

Halprin, Sara. *"Look at My Ugly Face!" Myths and Musings on Beauty and Other Perilous Obsessions with Women's Appearance*. New York: Penguin Books, 1995.

Hesse-Biber, Sharlene. *Am I Thin Enough Yet? The Cult of Thinness and the Commercialization of Beauty*. New York: Oxford University Press, 1996.

*Hirschmann, Jane R. and Munter, Carol H. *When Women Stop Hating Their Bodies: Freeing Yourself from Food and Weight Obsession*. New York: Fawcett Columbine, 1995.

*Hillman, Carolynn. *Love Your Looks: How to Stop Criticizing and Start Appreciating Your Appearance*. New York: Simon & Schuster, 1996.

Hollis, Judi. *Fat and Furious: Women and Food Obsession*. New York: Ballantine Books, 1994.

Hollis, Judi. *Fat Is a Family Affair*. San Francisco: HarperCollins Publishers, 1985.

*Johnston, Joni E. *Appearance Obsession: Learning to Love the Way You Look*. Deerfield Beach, FL: Health Communications, Inc., 1994.

*Kano, Susan. *Making Peace with Food: Freeing Yourself from the Diet/Weight Obsession*. New York: Harper & Row Publishers, 1989.

Lee-Thorpe, Karen. *Why Beauty Matters*. Colorado Springs: NavPress, 1997.

Maine, Margo. *Father Hunger: Fathers, Daughters & Food*. Carlsbad, CA: Gurze Books, 1991.

Meadow, Rosalyn M. and Weiss, Lillie. *Good Girls Don't Eat Dessert*. New York: Harmony Books, 1992.

Morrison, Andrew P. *The Culture of Shame*. New York: Ballantine Books, 1996.

Pipher, Mary. *Hunger Pains: What Every Woman Needs to Know about Food, Dieting, and Self-Concept*. Holbrook, MS: Adams Publishing, 1995.

Pipher, Mary. *Reviving Ophelia: Saving the Selves of Adolescent Girls*. New York: Ballantine Books, 1994.

Riebel, Linda and Kaplan, Jane. *Someone You Love Is Obsessed with Food: What You Need to Know About Eating Disorders*. Center City, MN: Hazeldon Educational Materials, 1989.

Roth, Geneen. *Appetites: On the Search for True Nourishment*. New York: Dutton, 1996.

Roth, Geneen. *When Food Is Love: Exploring the Relationship Between Eating and Intimacy*. New York: Penguin Books, 1992.

Rusk, Tom and Read, Randy. *I Want to Change but I Don't Know How!* New York: Price Stern Sloan, Inc., 1986.

Sanford, Linda Tschirhart and Donovan, Mary Ellen. *Women & Self-Esteem: Understanding and Improving the Way We Think and Feel about Ourselves*. New York: Penguin Books, 1984.

Schwartz, Hillel. *Never Satisfied: A Cultural History of Diets, Fantasies and Fat*. New York: Doubleday, 1986.

Székely, Éva. *Never Too Thin*. Toronto: The Women's Press, 1988.

Wolf, Naomi. *The Beauty Myth: How Images of Beauty Are Used Against Women*. New York: Doubleday, 1991.

AUTHOR

Judith Couchman is the owner of Judith & Company and works full-time as an author, speaker, and editorial consultant. She is the author/compiler of fifteen books, including *The Woman Behind the Mirror*, *Shaping a Woman's Soul*, and *Designing a Woman's Life*. Before starting her own company, she was the founding editor-in-chief of *Clarity*, a national magazine for Christian and spiritually seeking women.

With over twenty years in the publishing industry, Judith has served as director of product development for NavPress periodicals, director of communications for The Navigators, editor of *Sunday Digest* and managing editor of *Christian Life*. In these capacities she has talked with women around the country, through formal and informal research, giving her deep insight and an original perspective on meeting their spiritual needs. She has also worked as a public relations practitioner, a free-lance reporter, and a high school journalism teacher, and has earned an M.A. in journalism and a B.S. in education.

Judith has received national awards for her work in religious publishing, corporate communications, and secondary education, and speaks to women's and professional groups around the country. She lives in Colorado and when time permits, studies art history at a local college.

Visit Judith Couchman's website at
http://www.judithcouchman.com
to learn more about her books.

To schedule Judith to speak to your group, contact:

CLASServices, Box 66810, Albuquerque, NM 87193, 505-899-4283 phone; 505-899-9282 fax.